COLLECTED BOYHOOD WORKS
Volume Four

POETIC REMINISCENCES

BOOK OF DISLOCATION

LYRICS AND OTHER TRADITIONAL LONGER POEMS

Udenta O. Udenta

Published by
Kraft Books Limited
6A Polytechnic Road, Sango, Ibadan
Box 22084, University of Ibadan Post Office
Ibadan, Oyo State, Nigeria
✆ +234 (0)803 348 2474, +234 (0)805 129 1191
E-mail: kraftbooks@yahoo.com
Website: www.kraftbookslimited.com

© Udenta O. Udenta, 2015

First published 2015

ISBN 978–978–918–229–9 (Paperback)
ISBN 978–978–918–278–0 (Hardback)

= KRAFTGRIOTS =
(A literary imprint of Kraft Books Limited)

All Rights Reserved

First printing, February 2015

Dedication

Rosy dawn of upspring game,
Dancing within the tone of golden dame,
Your godliness strikes like piercing bow,
Thy good naturedness creating a mass of abyss

5. Dawn into the oblivion of painless death,
   Beckoning, welcomes all to void of space,
   The spasmodic shudder, like eerie sound
   Thou caring boldly to create something new,
   I laughed during the spring or summer.

10. Receding gorgeously towards the depth of heart,
    Over my mysterious depth of uncertainties,
    The golden bloom reveals strong-willed helpers,
    Vultures hovering, striking with their tangled talons
    Long throats withholding incredible upspring.

15. Along the groovy avenue, you were never found wanting,
    Like the pure crag orb or the moon,
    Dancing vividly, seeing, comparing to soothing
    Beam, glowing silvery form latches me into
    Great chicken heart

20. Sounds well with crashing shell,
    Sweeping away acts of laziness
    Brushing aside uproots of haunting stump,

25. Great companions endangering evil emotion.
    To me countenance of flaming fire
    Shining brightly, bashing shadows of gloom,
    Letting not the doom of damp to fall,
    The glorious inheritance, litters of weight

30. Thinkers of old, assuming the fox's wiliness,
    Full of gaits of dewy groove,
    The joy of austere contemplation's metallic agony dwindling
    Merrily, laughing scorn vanishing into thin air,

35. Laughter or hope gaining fast on you,
    Wishers of ill-luck clambering for safety,
    Again, I greet,
    My heart yearning to live, illusion-some,

40. With burning daring, aware of the mourning labyrinths,
    high Harp of Apollo,
    The cymbal of Aeolion,
    The wonderment of Zephyr

45. Athena's golden eyes,
    Hera's hawk's nose, lyre of
    Mulls, ALL of you to inherit, loved
    Ones, securing the gate of eternity,
    Loving to be remembered by,

50. A darling great loved one

Author's Note

The volume four of the collected works contains three works: *Poetic Reminiscences, Book of Dislocation,* and *Lyrics and Other Traditional Longer Poems*, all collections of poetry. The works owe a lot to my study of English poetry, particularly the poetry of Wordsworth, Byron, Tennyson, Arnold and Coleridge and my knowledge of Igbo mythic tales. They were written in frank, though poor, imitation of romantic poetry, *Poetic Reminiscences* most especially. Another remarkable feature of the first two collections is the deep passion I had, and still have, for classical Greek mythology and the, sometimes, curious use I made of the myths and legends I learned. Some of the poems in the first two collections are suffused with mythic allusions, images and motifs, oftentimes, applied outside their cultural and environmental contexts!

However, *Book of Dislocation,* and *Lyrics and Other Traditional Longer Poems* are series of poetic reflections on various subjects- traditional, modern, social, metaphysical, transcendental, mythic and moral. The two collections are more mature than *Poetic Reminiscences* and show a maturing, independent poetic imagination increasingly able to creatively domesticate and adapt universal mythic and poetic consciousness to specific African, nay, Igbo cultural setting. They must have been one of the last works I wrote, probably between late 1978 and early 1979. Another point worth making here is that they were never completed, as indicated on their original handwritten version, including the covers of the exercise books in which they were composed.

Udenta O. Udenta
Abuja, March 2014

Prologue

The golden flower of happiness blooms,
The saturated scent piercing black void,
Smelling rottenly, still languishing happily,
The time is reset, ready for action,
5   Against the damp of gloomy dawn,
      Striving gallantly, settling problems of conscience,
      Alas! A great evil has happened,
      So full the curse, sediments of sorrow

10   A huge snake glided in, hacking the hooves, swelling of
      Hatched chicks,
      What remains, falling from chimpanzee post,
      The root of life trying to vanish,

15   Astute moody nature laughing scornfully,
      Its spectacular sense, ecstasy of sorrow
      The rapture treasures not troubled heart
      Exertion of energy, vial of hopelessness
      I wonder the hope of survival.

20   Suddenly it cracks down, pouring rain drops.
      It rains on my tears, clearing the brow,
      The red flashes brilliantly
      Heaving against the feisty air

25   It was done with burning unhappiness,
      Glory of many, blossoms all
      Chiming my life, releasing prophetic out-letting
      The sweet melody of winds constant,
      As intractable as the Northern Star,

30   Descending Oh! Descending down into
      Valley of hope
      Where? The withered land recovers celestially,
      Alone with the world I treasure,
      My hope lying at the Almighty's feet,

35   A wonderful show he reveals it to me,
      Whereof, the bungling seizure of life,
      Panging heart, dwindling violent beat,
      The regular pulse fluttering metaphorically,
      Ancient ancestral blunders,

40   Blabbing merrily, ushering good love,
      THEY composed poems of tragedy,
      The love of world matters naught,
      Save for love itself
      Succumbing down – deep chasm, the

45   Hallow of hallows – the shoal of hell,
      The bloody, angry souls springing,
      Devouring – I placating, unearthly
      Beasts, fluttering the golden broom
      Blackness worsens, by mysterious shape,

50   The songs of welcome – echoes,
      Re-echoing tragically,
      Interchanging course by the outer way,
      Match-flare of anger swelling your body
      As lineage welcomes with harsh solace

55   Slowing down, down flow
      Streaming well with red of
      Blood – enjoy all happiness,
      Or mortal world, crying now
      No escape track, covered
      With thorn, trailing your course

60   Quadrangle of evil reflecting not my way,
      The glorious song of joy immortal,
      Blending favourably, hearkening deeply
      It advanced, stretched and grasped,

65 Captures firmly with swaggering zeal,
    The plaintive rays, arrowing dawn,
    So also the brightening of the gloomy dawn
    A liberty of laughter,
    The song of Apollo's lyrical rite

70 The grove of Athena's booming volcano, thundering
    Her golden Pallas myth
    The chamber of split, All
    Aiding, sharpening my sword,
    Watching doefully, meekness and mirth,

75 A mean rush of curiosity,
    Dwarfing, dwindling firmly, evil emotion,
    The time of ripened glory, intensively –
    The period of joy, the movement of
    Merriment,

80 Long-snouted rocks of demons,
    Above all, of evil mythology,
    I brushed them aside
    A simple truth
    Deep it was, even in damnation,
    Evil passion, the compassion of love

85 The passion of joy,
    Pathetic cry, rising gently from immortal
    Heart,
    The magic of Eupherius
    The wileness of Odysseus

90 Achilles' gallant and valorous stand,
    The bulging heart of Ajax, full of fire,
    The mighty fleet of the Myrmidons
    The vast empire of Menelaus
    And Agamemnon

95 The wisdom par excellence of Old King Nestor,
    All inherited, possessed and craved,
    Rejoice! The time is reset near, at hand
    The attained goal is at hand also

      Craving bushes, long-limbed
100 Far flung owl's den,
      Barking of dogs, All Amusing,
      The myth of the future,
      Prevailing like quivering bow,
      Full of mystery, uncertainties,

105 The contentment of good hope,
      Wondering about nothing new,
      Quivering sound, hallowing near
      The trumpet of heaven,
      The choir of immortal fame,

110 Aflame the golden azure
      The astute life and living,
      The Joy of heaven, the song of angels
      Piercing, crying, beckoning, calling

115 All cravers of material wealth,
      Possessors of earthly treasure,
      No storage for deathless fame.
      All good worshipers, calling you,
      Down – down – all crowning you,
      Marching leaders to eternity,

120 The guide of triumphant entry,
      Leading like flickering pilot light,
      Advancing onward, deserting, dwarfing,
      All sharp stumps of obstruction,
      But loo! The to-wit-twat cry,

125 All along the thicket of thorny path,
      Obstinate beings embracing you,
      Groping dawn, hurrying to satanic
      Palace,
      Sitting, crowned for centuries,

130 Awake and punch the bloody Scamander,
      The evil tribulation, Trojan massacre,
      Hark of stone, creepers of demon forest,

      Story of granite blow,
      Watch on, read deep, take much,

135 Obedience of soothsayers, seers,
      Bidding away, protruding,
      The vapour of dawn,
      The mist of pregnant morning
      Thousand stars of sunny joy

140 Welcoming the grumpy morning
      Light sparkled scene, the
      Visibility of harmlessness,
      Meekly, humbly, gently, slowly – steady
      But firm, full of volcanic rockets

145 Out-lettings of vapour, pieces of jagged
      Rock,
      Bombs of composite eruption,
      All alike, together, joining
      Squeezing, bending, yielding,

150 Mingling savagely, going
      Down, deep together to abyss,
      Of yawning caves

Contents

Dedication	5
Author's Note	7
Prologue	8
General Introduction to the Volumes	15
Poetic Reminiscences	**31**
Snapshots of Ancient Ways	32
Risky Ship Journey	36
Pushing to the Unknown	37
Suffering – Poor's Way	38
True Love Sees Nothing Bad	39
My Loving Heart Saved Me	40
Easy – Round Way	41
Tribute to Departed Friends	42
Destruction of Evil Forces	43
The Price of Recklessness	45
Unforgettable	47
Ishirikpam	50
Down to Mortals	51
Goodness of the World	52
Beautiful Heavenly Paradise	53
Foolishness and its likely Repercussion	54
Rain	55
Pushing the Bridge of Stone	57
Price of Immorality and Illegal Acquisition	59
Unshakable Rock	61
Voices of the Sea, Legend, Thunder	63
Fox in Sheep's Skin	64
Fools	68

Visible Power of Darkness and Light	69
Captives	70
Indemnity of Hell	71
Debt of Sorrow	73
Great Ancestors	75
Obstinate Pones	76
Trapped	78
Caricature Sickness	80
Impossible Trial	81
Sacrificial Sheep	82
Hopeless Whited Sepulchre	83
The Coming of Riverine Flocks	84
Lack of Understanding	85
Away with the Contented Heart	86
Suffer my People Naught	87
Land of Pleasure	89
Long – Throaty Vultures	91
Worthlessness	92
Crushed To Pieces	93
Obedient Little Blush	95
Too Strong to Punish	96
Salvation of Mortals	98
Peril in Dreamland	99
Vengeance is mine	101
"Aerodim" (Plane)	105
Departed Ones, Great Judges	106
Shining Moon – Daughter of Heaven	110
Book of Dislocation	**115**
Mystery of Disappearance – Blown up	116
Prologue	119
Where are the Illegally bought Fighters?	129
Woman Nature - Cursable	132
The Vengeful One, I Once Knew Him	134
Lyrics and Other Traditional Longer Poems	**137**

General Introduction to the Volumes

I have thought long and hard about publishing these volumes of short stories, novels, drama sketches, essays, philosophical musings and other materials of an inter-generic nature written between 1977 and 1979, when I was in high school. All the works in these six volumes were written when I was between the ages of 13 and 15. On very many occasions in the past, I have dismissed the thought of ever publishing these materials, rightly considering them immature, full of linguistic, structural and stylistic inadequacies and, thus capable of sending the wrong kind of signal to better equipped and far more talented teenagers about how best not to nurse, conceive and execute their creative impulses and inspiration.

However, I am now more than convinced that these works should see the light of day, precisely because they meant much to me when they were written, and may be much more now as I cast my mind back to the socio-cultural and spatio-temporal determinations in which they inher. I am also persuaded that my bad English, bad grammar and immature ideas and vision are not an exception to the creative enterprise and pursuits of young people of my age when I wrote them; and that given the opportunities and possibilities open to me, and the obstacles I have had to overcome in creating them, their own creative productions may not be too far higher or lower than my effort.

It will be thus necessary to situate these works within the context of my historical, social, cultural and other sources of identity and motivations, believing that a glimpse into these currents will help place them in their proper and objective psycho-social setting.

My father, Chief Benedict Ikenche Udenta, who died in 2004,

was a trained teacher whose vacation job was to help his elder brothers tap and sell palm wine. By dint of hard work, unique talent and special intellectual gift and drive, he was able to finish his teachers training programme at the famous St. Charles College, Onitsha, Nigeria, earned a Teacher Grade One Certificate subsequently and completed his B.Sc. Inter from the University of London in 1963 or thereabout, the very year I was born.

He broke away from the mission school system because of its overbearing and constricting spiritual-dogmatic conditions, codes and circumstances, which he felt hampered and limited his intellectual growth and liberal disposition and philosophy; taught in a number of secondary and commercial colleges; helped in starting and sustaining the tradition of publishing at Tabansi Publishing Ltd that flourished in the 1960s; wrote and published nearly 20 books; contested for the Federal House of Representatives for the Awgu-Oji River Federal Constituency under the banner of the Dr. K.O. Mbadiwe-led Democratic People's National Congress (DPNC) in 1959; bought a Volkswagen Beetle convertible car that helped in many a local wedding; and erected a storey building in 1963. He made all these accomplishments when he was about 32 or 33 years.

My mother, Madam Pauline Ijeabalum Udenta, who is still alive, complemented my father in virtually all respects. She trained as nurse/midwife at the famous Bishop Shanaham School of Nursing and Midwifery, Nsukka, Nigeria, and practiced for a while in government health institutions before her husband's "opposition politics" in DPNC forced her out of government service into private practice, a calling that she still responds to till date. Her greatest strength is her profound understanding and accommodation of her husband's intellectual and creative disposition and her complete tolerance, love and support for him in the pursuit of what may have then appeared a strange cause. Till the very end of his life, even as his health failed, still struggling gallantly with his reading, research and writing (he became increasingly attracted to mystical philosophy in the last decade and half of his life, essentially as an intellectual pursuit, and not as a devotee, though he compiled by hand and typed over 500 spiritual and mystical prayers for the family), she never ceased to encourage him, though would occasionally take the books and papers away and direct his minds to other things, more so as he found a particular joy in reading the Catholic publication, **Preparation for Death,** in the months leading to his passing away.

The combination of a thoroughly intellectual, even philosophic father who wrote the bulk of his books between his mid-twenties and early thirties, and a very intelligent mother who became increasingly anchored on the same path of social liberalism and tolerance of contrary viewpoints, eventually produced four children who expressed their individual creativity and intellectual consciousness in various ways. Because of their years of travels in places far and wide in the old Anambra State of Nigeria, the children never had the consciousness of growing up in our ancestral, rural village of Mgbowo in Awgu L.G. of Enugu State, Nigeria before the end of the civil war in 1970.

It was thus to this village setting that we journeyed towards the end of 1969, across strange places and lands, on foot and with varied, interesting and exciting, though frightening experiences, to aid our passage. The rest of the family traveled first, while our father followed later, after creating safe passages for us across the hostile, twisting routes with messages of our coming delivered ahead to his comrades in the Biafran Organization of Freedom Fighters (BOFF), an irregular, guerilla army, that became the backbone of the Biafran resistance even after the conventional fighting force had disintegrated, but a force which was under-funded and under-appreciated by a military command structure that seemed completely uninformed about the tactics and strategies of an unconventional warfare.

Till date, I still marvel at the comments made by my father on the margins of virtually all the pages of Chairman Mao's **Essays on Military Warfare** which he had with him every day of the war, and which I read (the Essays and the comments) – during my high school days; comments which demonstrated the great parallels between the conditions of the struggle of the Chinese Communists and the Biafran resistance fighters, but a wide divergence between the brilliant Chinese communist responses and the inept and ill-conceived strategies of the Biafran commanding officers.

As we settled in our rural environment amidst the ruins of war, shattered hopes and broken homes and dreams, and in a 12-bedroom house whose lower floor was carpeted by dried excreta left behind by departing soldiers, and whose library had been used as screwed up tissue papers, it did occur to me that my earliest artistic impressions and, probably, the first formative ingredients of my creativity were deeply rooted in those special nights at Utu, near Nnewi, in both moon-laden and star-lit nights, and other nights of forbidden gloom and threatening thunder, as my father's BOFF comrades foregathered, drinking gin and singing songs of war, bravery and heroism. My love for poetry, drama and storytelling must have been formed then, as a 5 or 6 year-old, and till date I can still recite all those Biafran war songs which I memorized at heart and many of which were later celebrated by Chukwuemeka Ike in **Sunset at Dawn**.

Every family is a unique creation and has a unique identity. It expresses itself as a life force in a special manner with sets of communicable ethos, values and ideals never to be found exactly in other households.

For me, the peculiar, unique expression of our family identity lay in the effortless ease with which communication was carried out and shared, with candour, passion and contestation of ideas at every turn. Both my parents are totally liberal in their understanding of family relations and child upbringing. Even as elementary school pupils, our voices were to be heard loud and clear, from the upper floor to the main road just across the way, as we engaged our parents in impassioned discussions about life and reality. Friends and neighbours would always marvel at and comment about the "strange behaviour" of the Udentas who never seemed to cease talking and maybe arguing or disputing with one another.

Yet, a great spectacle awaited them at the sense of love, family devotion, loyalty, bond and commitment, and the near fierce and fanatical hero-worshipping by children of their parents. For in spite of our being bold at the discussion table, especially as we grew older and matured – a situation that almost always produced six varied points of view – we saw in them the reflection of God on earth and obeyed, respected and honoured them as good children were wont to.

This liberal parental disposition encouraged the flowering of personal potentials and self-expression, an attitude that we took to the extreme, sometimes, but now happily with no serious negative consequences. The oldest of us children, Fidelia, entered high school when the rest of us boys were still in elementary school, and during holidays, our sister being very sociable, extroverted and lively, our home became one of the social meeting centres and points of interaction for college boys, with music, dance, drinks and cigarettes in the mix. Music was supplied by my father's old gramophone player, whose sound production my immediate elder brother, Ben Jr., ingenuously increased by placing the speakers atop a large earthenware pot so as to produce the then popular resounding bass overlay.

Social parties, then called "pop", were to be held in our house or in some other liberal households, with the 45 rpm discs supplied, believe it or not, by our mother, whose fortnightly trips to Enugu to purchase drugs and other medical supplies for her maternity, also included the purchase of "pop" music carefully written down by my sister and eldest brother, Okey Maurice, with a charge that she should not come back unless all the discs in the list were bought!

Our music experience was formed by the burgeoning post-war pop music culture spawned by such creative geniuses and artistes as Jonathan Udensi (Spud Nathans), Manfred Best and Jerry Boifriand of the **Wings** (The group later split into two with the tragic death of Spud Nathans – arguably the best pop vocalist in the history of Nigerian pop music – with Best leading the **Original Wings** and Jerry Boifrand leading the **Super Wings**); Chyke Fusion and **The Apostles; Founder's 15; Black children; One World; Cloud 7;** Tony Grey; **Semi-colon;** Sunny Okosuns; Bongos Ikwue; **Blo**; Lijadu Sisters; and Ofege. Later, **Sweet Breeze** (some of whose leading members were my sister's schoolmates at IMT, Enugu); Chris Okotie; Jide Obi; and Christy Essien-Igbokwe were to become an intergral part of this rich musical and cultural exposure and experience. On the traditional side were **The Oriental Brothers,** Osadebe and the Peacocks International Band.

On reflection, I can justifiably say that our family environment and culture, our parents' liberalism, tolerance and understanding, and their expectation that we will and must eventually find our way and purpose in life made us live our life to the full, sometimes, in excess of social pursuits, far ahead of our age. On balance, it is to their greater glory and honour that we turned out right, and more than repaid their confidence in us.

My eldest sister, Fidelia Nkire, is married to Hon. Sam Nkire, a one-time commissioner in Abia State, a presidential ambassadorial nominee, a former member of a major federal board and presently the national chairman of one of Nigeria's leading political parties, the Progressive People's Alliance. Of their four children, the eldest, Queenette is presently pursuing her Masters degree in London. My eldest brother, Okey Maurice, is an accomplished and successful businessman who lives with his wife, Irene, and three daughters in Enugu. My immediate elder brother, Ben Junior, not long ago relocated to Abuja with his wife and three sons from their base at Abingdom, Maryland, USA.

As for me, the last born, I can equally claim a measure of self-attainment; having left university teaching as a Senior Lecturer; being a leading figure in the pro-democracy movement that resisted the late General Sani Abacha's tyranny; having served as the founding National Secretary of Alliance for Democracy, AD; and was until Dec. 2009 a Director in a Presidential Peace Building Institute.

I have gone into this relatively detailed account about how we, the children, turned out for, often times, I do reflect on what the situation could or may have been given the liberalism of our parents, their tolerance and even open, joyful acceptance of our vision of life and our place in it, and the unconditional allowance they gave us in choosing our careers and life partners. It was a balancing act that was successfully negotiated, and I strongly believe that if they had not attained the height they did, where upon we drew our inspiration, drive and motivation, maybe, that act would not have been well balanced.

However, let me quickly add that I can now, in retrospect, see something of their social strategy. While our parents were liberal in intellectual matters and social situations that connect us to others, they were strict disciplinarians in matters domestic. Our father may not speak out for months on end; his very commanding and influential presence was enough condition for order to reign. If it did get out of hand, as was the case usually with boys, and a boisterous girl of the ages of 8 -12, a smack or two from his cane would cause peace to reign for weeks on end.

Our mother, on the other hand, as most mothers are often given to perform, always had her hand to aid her tongue as she instilled family discipline and compliance to family tasks and responsibilities of orderliness, hardwork, diligence and obedience virtually on hourly basis. It may be correct to stress that the combination of social and intellectual liberalism and permissiveness with strict enforcement of discipline and good conduct at the home front, in domestic situations, may be the objective force that helped in tilting the scale in favour of the relative success we have all made of our lives.

My first recollection of school was a low, mud walled, thatched-roof, rectangular building that leaked very badly when it rained. The door way was always wet, soggy and damp. The open space in front of the building always ran with sluggish water and debris, especially along the gutters. I could also picture millipedes squirming in and out of the soggy earth. For one reason or the other my mind was never fully given to the words of the teacher or the activities inside the "classroom", but was always constantly centred on the wet earth around me, the squirming millipedes, in blind, terror-ridden fascination. While it always seemed to rain in my recollection, I cannot say. This was at Utu, probably, around mid-1969.

When my family eventually settled at our ancestral village of Mgbowo in 1970, my "classroom" was only slightly better. I started Elementary One again, under a huge mango tree that dominated the entrance to Central School Mgbowo, with its gnarled, exposed roots serving as our seats. But schooling in the village was a beautiful experience. Recitations of verses were a regular occurrence during the morning assembly, and so also were the numerous singing lessons that heralded the end of a school year or the graduation of Elementary Six pupils. I enjoyed those singing sessions and the learning of alphabets, rendered in a song-like fashion. I enjoyed also the sense of illumination and expansion of the imagination engendered by a particularly inspired social studies teacher whose name I have forgotten but who we all collectively owed our knowledge of the world and current affairs as he spoke eloquently yet under another mango tree that he preferred to instruct us probably in our elementary four or five.

The choice of this tree was deliberate by him, for by then the classrooms had been equipped with desks and chairs, yet he preferred to fire our youthful imagination outside the confines of a classroom block, insisting instead that we commune with nature outside. I guess my love for nature, of plants, trees and animals, and my passion for politics and world affairs were formed then.

Our after school experiences, especially during long vacations, exemplified the poetry of living in a rural environment. We hunted rats, lizards, bush rabbits, and grass cutters, set traps for crabs in muddy patches leading to the village streams, and for birds that ate up the maize in the farm. We swam inside the muddy waters of the streams and fished with anything we could lay hands on, sometimes, with such a deadly chemical as gamalin 20, the purchase of which I had the honour or dishonour of undertaking, being the last born and the most innocent-looking. We picked wild berries, 'Icheku', locusts and the lava or pupa of butterflies that infested the village breadfruit trees.

Opportunities to read abounded in our house. My father gradually rebuilt his library and began subscribing to **Awake**, the Jehovah Witnesses publication; a venture that ultimately produced over 30 bound volumes in the 1980s and 1990s. Till date my love for **Awake** never abated, and I still acquire the odd copy or two, every now and then. I cannot now fully recollect all that I read from my father's fairly large stock of books, but as I gradually grew older and entered high school, I did recall that between classes two or three and five, I had read, several times over, Will Durant's **The Story of Philosophy,** and **The History of Political Thought** (the author of who I cannot recollect, and a book my father, on a particular occasion, took away from me, pointing out that it was far too mature for my age).

That must have been in my class three or four. I also formed my first impressions about Marxism and communism by reading a short, introductory series published by Western scholars, and dealing with a critique of Lenin's positions on several subjects: **Lenin and Imperialism, Lenin on the State and Revolution, Lenin and the National Question,** etc. I also read from his rich stock of English and American poetry books, and his own writings.

Being a boarding student in a village secondary school (I attended Awgu County Secondary School, later renamed Awgu High School, Nenwe, Awgu L.G.A. in Enugu State, which was established in 1958 when county colleges flourished, and which must have had its high points in the 1960s before the war, but which suffered the fate many a school in Eastern Nigeria suffered after the war: decay of infrastructure, poor funding, poor staffing, etc), which was a mere 3 kilometres from my village of Mgbowo, afforded me some opportunities for intellectual growth and the nursing of the creative spirit.

We had a crop of teachers (my father had just left the school in 1975 as I was entering it to take up a post as an Education Officer in the local government headquarters), who were dedicated, who knew their stuff and who were prepared to go the extra mile, limited facilities notwithstanding, to impart as much knowledge on us as they possibly could.

My love for books and reading, which was already deeply entrenched during my elementary school days, grew stronger when I entered secondary school. I recollect being appointed the Librarian of class 1C, my class, or probably the librarian of the whole class, and finding myself spending long hours soaking up as much as I could in the serene environment of the school library. I read virtually the whole works of Enid Blyton, particularly **The Famous Five** series. I read the poetry of Lord Alfred Tennysson, Matthew Arnold, Lord Byron, Alexander Pope, and the American Transcendentalists. I also read Caryle's **Classical Myths, Myths and Legends of Ancient Greece, Classical Myths in Song and Story,** and different versions of Homer's **Iliad** and **The Odyssey**.

I can also recall that I read a particular volume of **The Encyclopedia Britannica** which I enjoyed but found very difficult to understand, the works of Shakespeare (the drama texts, his sonnets and the stories derived from the drama texts), and some African novels. My hometown being only 40 kilometres from Enugu, I found myself making weekly journeys to purchase novels and other creative works under the African writers series edition (I did pride myself that I read virtually all the works in the series in print and available in book stores in Enugu before I left high school), and such socialist publications as **New Dawn, Socialism: Theory and Practice** and **Socialism: Principles, Practice and Prospects.** I also bought and read all the novels of James Hadley Chase and Nick Carter available in Enugu (indeed my nickname as a high school student was Kill Master: Nick Carter's secret service rating no, and a name that my high school mates and friends still call me till this date). I also bought and read all the writings of Tuesday Lobsang Rampa, including his most definitive work, *I Believe*, apart from **The Third Eye, Doctor from Lhasa,** etc. All these were in addition to buying and reading virtually all the novels and stories in the Pacesetter series and Mills and Boon series, and also as many novels of Barbara Cartland, Denise Robbins and Harold Robbins that I could lay my hands on.

My youthful imagination and creative desire were also fired by such prescribed reading texts in classes one and two in high school; Chinua Achebe's **Chike and the River,** Cyprian Ekwensi's **The Drummer Boy, An African Night's Entertainment** and **The Passport of Mallam Illia** (I read **Burning Grass** which I found difficult and hard-going, **Jagua Nana** and **People of the City** on my own); Onuora Nzekwu and Michael Crowther's **Eze Goes to School** (the most popular and influential of the prescribed texts); **Trouble in Form Five; One Week, One Trouble; The Adventures of Souza;** Anezi Okoro's **New Broom at Amanzu** and **The Village Headmaster,** and very many others.

The list of the African novels in the African Writers Series that left indelible mark in my mind and helped to germinate any creative impulses in my class two-four include: Chinua Achebe's

Things Fall Apart, ***No Longer at Ease***, ***Arrow of God*** and ***A Man of the people;*** Wole Soyinka's ***The Interpreters*** (which I found very difficult); Amu Djoleto's ***The Strange Man***; Stanlake Samkange's ***On Trial For My Country;*** and Kenneth Kaunda's ***Zambia Shall Be Free*** (probably the most popular African autobiography among the students, with the possible exception of Achebe's ***Things Fall Apart).*** Ngugi wa Thiong'o's ***Weep Not Child*** was hugely popular among students, so also his **The River Between** and ***A Grain of Wheat.*** The same could be said of *John Munonye's* ***The Only Son*** and ***Obi*** (I was to read his ***A Bridge to a Wedding*** and **The Oil Man of Obange** as a student of English and Literary Studies at the University of Nigeria, Nsukka); Onuora Nzekwu's **My Mercedes is Bigger Than Yours**; Obi B. Egbuna's ***Diary of a Homeless Prodigal*** (which inspired one of the texts in this volume), ***Elina*** and ***The Madness of Didi;*** T.M. Aluko's ***One Man, One Wife*** (another very popular novel with students) and ***One Man, One Machete.*** (I was eventually to read virtually all his other novels as a university student, including **His Worshipful Majesty** and **Chief The Honourable Minister*);*** and Chukwuemeka Ike's **Sunset at Dawn** and **The Potter's Wheel** which made a great impression on me as a high school student. I was to eventually read his **The Naked Gods, Toads for Supper, The Chicken Chasers, Expo '77** and his other novels as a university student.

These are some of the novels, stories, drama works, etc that I still recollect having read in high school. I not only read them, but bought them. However, as was usually the case, I eventually lost most of them; though I have made tremendous effort to re-stock my library with all these books and more. The list of the materials I read was surely far longer than the listing above, but I have captured some of them as a way of demonstrating the sources of my creative vision and the way and manner that my imagination was fired. Readers of these volumes will see, note and observe that some of my boyhood works were influenced by some of these books, and that echoes of them, direct and, sometimes, very dangerous, abound in the volumes.

Yet, in spite of what one can call the preparation of the mind

I was a very bad student in my classes one and two. At the end of each term, and during promotion examinations, I always found myself toward the tail end of the class. The reason may have been the distraction caused by my absorption with extra-curricular reading materials, but also being the last born, with two older brothers who were in the same school, I must have felt over-sheltered and over-protected that it took me sometime before I could find my independent feet and allow my natural endowments and talents to flower and flourish.

I became a better student in my class three, and may have been the best student during the promotion examinations from class four to class five, a feat that earned me the honour of being appointed a study prefect for class one and two students, and the whole school librarian. By the end of my class four I had read the WASC syllabus maybe three or four times over and, to all intents and purposes, was fully ready then for the WASC and JAMB examinations. Indeed, I took the JAMB examination in the second term of form five and was the second candidate admitted to read English at UNN. It was while already in the university that the WASC results came out, confirming my status as a university student.

And in full consultation with a number of my school mates, my brother Ben Jr., Austine Okeke, Charles Okeke, Emmanuel Akpa, the late Chris Aju, Anayo Simon Agu (who was the school senior prefect) and Patrick Isiogwu, I virtually stopped attending classes for the whole of Form Five, declaring in my youthful exuberance that those who really desire knowledge already have it; the passing of English, Chemistry and Physics, etc being not dependent on Grieve and Pratt, Lambert and Nelkon, etc respectively!

Interestingly, I did extremely well in the WASC mock examinations (I recollect scoring A1 in about 7 or 8 subjects, and together with Aju and Patrick Isiogwu, defied our history teacher's belief that no student will score A1 in his mock examination, by all scoring A1 + in same). Virtually all my closest schoolmates passed the main WASC examinations with either a Division 1 or a good Division 2 level of pass.

I suspect that I began writing in earnest about the beginning of 1977 when I was in form two. I wrote consistently during the next two years or so, after school hours, late at night in various school classrooms, and especially during long vacations. In retrospect, I do believe that I may have enjoyed reading and writing to other social activities, including dancing, dating and hanging out with friends, but all these I did and enjoyed enormously, though on each occasion I would usually come back to continue from where I stopped.

My most productive creative years were 1977-1979. I do not think that I wrote much in 1980, the year I graduated from high school. I was, however, not alone in this creative pursuit. Who started it may never be known, but a fledging creative writing tradition was spawned among a few of us which led to a healthy rivalry and a positive spirit of competition and the search for excellence. Somehow or the other, the news filtered out that I was writing novels, drama sketches and such like. When I eventually let in my close friends what I was up to, read my writings to them and pasted same on a weekly basis, on the wall beside my corner at Akanu Ibiam Hostel, yet another story began making the rounds that our school senior prefect, Anayo Agu who is now with the American Embassy in Lagos but who we all called Asasi Agu, was also into something very special.

It was soon discovered that he had conceived a mythopoeic interpretation of the essence of the mysterious water-maid with creative derivatives from "Omo" stream, a small, slow moving stream that bounded our school. He was to be seen at the bank of this stream, probably drawing inspiration from its inscrutable depths. Eventually, he came out with his prose-poetry work, called "Omodima," a creative piece that was peerless at the time.

While I may have been the most versatile and prolific in the range of genres I covered in my writings I was by no means the only writer around, and probably not even the best in terms of the maturity of vision and structure of presentation. Apart from Asasi Agu, the following classmates of mine also tried their hands in creative writing. My immediate elder brother, Ben Jr. wrote a beautiful novelette set in our village, maybe in response to the challenge set by my writings, which may have become a nuisance to him. The spirit of "I can do better than you" must have stimulated his creative consciousness and nudged his imaginative spirit for he, indeed, did craft an elegant work that none of mine ever dusted. The search for that manuscript continues and if seen, I do hope to convince him, Asasi Agu and the rest of them (if they can still find their manuscripts), to put out a companion volume to this series.

Engr. Emmanuel Akpa who works with PHCN, in Enugu also tried his hand in creative writing and editorial work. So did Patrick Isiogwu and the late Chris Aju, and maybe a few others whose names I cannot presently remember. It was, of course, not surprising that, with the exception of Emma Akpa, the rest of us were arts-based or inclined, and it was then something special for him, a science student, to hold his own very much in our midst. It was, again, not by accident that we all belonged to the debating society and represented the school at local, zonal and state-wide debating and quiz competitions.

The spirit of dialogue, debate, discourse, competition and friendly rivalry pervaded our academic and social space and urged us to greater heights of endeavour. It was principally this spirit, cast in a provincial, rural clime, but hot and passionate, in combination with the more pristine currents and forces that shaped my life and conditioned my personality and identity, that led to the creation of the works that I will be shortly introducing.

The works collected in these volumes are by no means the only ones I wrote when I was in high school. There are two others I can still remember but which are yet to be seen or discovered. One was a novel based in South Africa and dealt with the psychological trauma of a child growing up in the then apartheid enclave. It must have been inspired by my role as Ndaba in Tunji Fatilewa's play, **Torrents of Soweto**, a performance we put together for the School's Founder's Day Celebration. That must have been around November-December 1979, at the beginning of the first term of my form five. The second was a novelette based in an urban environment, the subject matter of which I cannot recollect, but I could still feel the images of my father, my mother, myself, my siblings and close friends in my consciousness of the text as I put these thoughts down.

One other comment worth making here is that as I tried to re-read all the works, one or two things stand out. Most of them were, alas badly or poorly written (a point I have already made) and reflected my immaturity in written English.

Secondly, because I read so much, I virtually forced out my ill-absorption of most of the works in my own creative productions.

Precisely because I wanted to command the use of English very powerfully and write as the masters of the language wrote, I used expressions anyhow, and on numerous occasions even invented my own words that apparently meant nothing! Readers of these volumes will see this difficult search by a yet to be fully formed mind that sought gallantly but sometimes vainly to create something out of his very fertile imagination and consciousness.

Again, because I will be making very short comments in the 'Author's Note' to each of the volumes, what is now left for me to do is to present their organizational and contentual structure. The six volumes which are presented below are:

1. Volume One
    i. **The Wrath of the Gods** – a novel

2. Volume Two
    i. **Book of Knowledge and Great Understanding** – extracts from several works, and original philosophical musings and social commentary
    ii. **Reflections on School Life** – an account of different aspects of secondary school life

3. Volume Three
    i. **Before They Came** – a novel

4. Volume Four
    i. **Poetic Reminiscences** – a collection of poems
    ii. **Book of Dislocation** – a collection of poems
    iii. **Lyrics and other Traditional Longer poems** – collection of poems.

5. Volume Five
   i. ***The Re-discovery of the Arlistoga*** – a detective/thriller novel
   ii. ***Retrospective Vision: Cultural Interactions*** – a collection of short stories
6. Volume Six
   i. **The Quarrel** (A Play)
   ii. **Chief Eze Isiagu's Troubles** (A Short Story)
   iii. **The Air Raid** (A Short Story)
   iv. **The Return of the People** (A Short Story)
   v. **Personality Clash in Hades** – part of a poetic drama
   vi. **Some Stories Told** – collection of short stories

    The above titles were the original ones I gave to the works, with the exception of the explanation separated by a dash. The titles are retained as I gave them when the works were written, even though why some of them were so titled, and what symbolism I had in mind, is anybody's guess.

    Finally, it is my hope and expectation that even though these works may not mean much to present-day mature, or even young readers, they were a part of my growing up and artistic and intellectual development, and a part of my history that I don't want lost. This is my modest defense in putting these volumes out; a defense that may appear weak to some, but which, nevertheless, points to a certain poignant, though grossly imperfect beginning, in consideration of the totality of my later intellectual productions.

Udenta O. Udenta
Abuja
February, 2014

Poetic Reminiscences

Snapshots of Ancient Ways

1. I came to the earth when lizards
   Were in ones and in twos
   When houses were built under the shade of ukwa tree,
   When the royal python was sacred
   When one part of the great evil oracle was still forming

   When the chameleon was learning
   How to walk,
   When the earth was not strong enough
   The child of Ngene and Njaa,
   The beautiful feathers of all time

2. I am eke, the sacred one that
   Made a great man to eat shit
   And also use his teeth to chew grass,
   The murderous ancestral spirits
   Which cause bellyache, and head
   Swelling
   A man who knows that he is not strong
   Enough should not offer fight for when
   It comes he produces premature shit.

   In the glowing misty figures of the
   Early morning light,
   In the thick cloud covered
   By dangerous smoke created by Nyang Dan,
   Capped in the thick, smoky, fiery
   Mist was the God of vengeance with the
   Ancient golden spear in his hand, seeking
   For his chance and the unfortunate
   Ones to slaughter

3. In the early days of Hupa, in the forest
   Where people have been thrown in
   The evil ground, appearing in the nightmare
   Of the wronged man, disturbing the quiet
   Sleep of unfortunate man, turning him to

Misty figures, closing the entrance of his
Wife's vagina and womb was the great
Sea god, Ikpokuta

4. In the days of ancestral Egwugwu
Spirits, when the monkeys were
Human beings
When rape was a common
Taboo among the underworld dwellers.
There appeared the old witch, an
Advanced woman who wiped out the whole race of Nridwarfs
in the face
Of the great blood rushing
Trees.
Young women were the object
Of bedding for the gods until
This old Gagol threw sentimental
Light on the face of the earth
There was a great bloodshed and
Slaughtering in the changing
Universe until the truth was told,
And agreement was made
And issued out between
The savers and the destroyers

5. In the deep ocean waters of the old
Clothed in the embroidered velvet of
Mystical men,
Piercing the thighs of
The innocent women
Roaming about in the early hours
Of the morning,
Carrying the cloaks of
Disease and vengeance,
Seeking the person
Who shed the royal blood
Of the father or the mother
Punishing the small children,
Were the Errinyes and the Sirens or the Sea Sirens

6. Carrying on their heads, covered
    With white shroud, was the dead body
    Of the secret society member
    Who their magician-head had taken,
    Following behind were the
    Black women of the society,
    Their ripe, maturing breasts dangling to and fro,
    In front of them.
    Their waists were only covered by leaves and beads,
    Leaving other parts of their body bare,
    Dancing, front and back, exposing
    Their private parts, were the women

7. Beyond the deep cracking skies of
    Death, the poor cries of the fatherless and motherless spiritual
    child could be distinguished
    From the teasings of the bush babies

    The great, momentous darkness raged
    Ordering episode after episode of the mystery
    Of the helpers who should be cared for
    In the small night with glowing fireflies,
    The children were behind the moon
    Trying to change to monkeys
    In fulfilment of the prophecy of old

    In the days when human beings
    Were immortals, when nothing
    Yes, nothing was tabooed

    The days when apemen and chimpanzees
    Were creeping, and were the same as mortals
    When the great humanistic innocence
    Was still under mythic construction.
    The days when the one-eyed giants
    Were still roaming the face of the earth.
    The days when 'Aku-bekee' was a sacrificial
    Instrument in the natural universe.

The days when also the poor creatures
Were wrecked, and were full of misery,
Beyond consolation, beyond redemption,
Yes, beyond salvation.

The helpless cries of the poor, parentless babies
Creaked through the stillness of darkness,
Until one day they will rise and punish their tormentors.

Risky Ship Journey

Crown the foaming vallies,
Groom the winding grove,
Like ship in float,
Gushing with the presence of

5. Dark wind, on the waters of brightness
   Hearken to the chronic strain
   Descending deep with clouds
   Over the spreading stars
   The hollow form, the rustle

10. Of wind, all roaring, the waves
    Dashes up the swell, rupturing
    The weathered throng
    Clinging to the gleaming current wind
    As they go on their airy journey

15. Mantle! Wooden mouth, shrieks!
    With horror, stump, blocks not like the
    Grassy plain
    Little with skimming tides
    The opinion of insane sea,

20. Not to allow its passage,
    Seeking whom to devour
    With thunder beam
    Bugs and fleas, horrible smell
    Like mice going up in flames

25. As the old sneering engine works
    Well to save the journeyers

Pushing to the Unknown

Things want to take another shape,
High crest of devil's house
You could not avoid the long throat,
And the claws of deathless immortals,

5. No tithe for life, nor life for renting,
   Shall the unpaid debt be cleared?
   Another moment to have,
   Stay all, for happiness or pleasure

10. Shall disappear in void or air,
    The hour of merriment with laughter
    Along the path long gone,
    Evil odours from smelly lions, surpassed
    The fantastic, incredible image

15. Of sorcery's palate,
    Nothingness out of this world,
    With clumsy, messy outlook,
    All longed for terrible deeds, but powerless they are
    Willful beings loosen not what is snared

20 Circulation of fresh young blood
    Running in trickle, like urinary spittle
     Heaved up the smell with the dainty
     Spirits

Suffering – Poor's Way

Forefront march men,
Lay crusts of fields and plains,
With attention in intensity
I, scorned by the power,

5.   Laughing like an insane one,
     They are willing with heavy weeping,
     To rest from frustration
     My gaze was powerful
     As ever as now, mumbling,

10   Of hysterical cries that ring the air,
     I stood expressionless watching
     The dramatic scene, like golden
     Vest of immortal crest
     Not Aphrodite, but nymph goddess

15.   Of strife, bull-like – so it seems
     What fates have in store for them
     Perchance–crumpling hearts,
     As streams of unchecked tears
     Rushed down my cheek

20   Alas! All are black, happiness
     Vanishing with metallic force,
     Monotonous rhythm of harps
     Little to salvage the harsh moment
     Of depression

25   All quaked deep, the rumbling
     Of gauzes over the low walls
     Sucking and seeking shelter
     Where the crazy ones fear to thread
     I considered the anxiety and

30   Muttered, "mortal world created for well-to-dos"

True Love Sees Nothing Bad

The revoking of love,
Was deep like torpedo
Embryo of compassion,
Mingled well without a word

5. Both melted and dissolved, forming,
   Lookers hurried away among windy tracks
   Mindless to the joy of the world
   I laughed at them but came not
   Alone

10. The avengers themselves waited for their turn
    Deep, heartily! Inside and swallow
    Up as it went again
    With warming works, longing in eyes

15. Never to shelter and looked dreamful
    'Twas plight, tingling as moist
    Scent of happy memory dashed
    Passed by to allow us enter.
    What could I say 'twas all about

20 Singing sirens even bent their
   Heads to see my passage
   Begotten was beyond human destination
   Where wanderers fail to step

25 Alas! High up the place,
   Where Aphrodite dwells
   Enjoying herself with deceived
   Mortals, but see my way as she deals,
   But see

30 True love, 'twas that lasts long enough
   And sees nothing wrong

My Loving Heart Saved Me

Along the tired, windy road,
With my spills, the art of knowledge,
The curse of questioning trifle
I advanced alone to satisfy my want

5.   Rushing in, I fell into it,
     Great ruler of power, much feared 'fore,
     Hot steams of unpoured blood
     Streaming down to love my tale,
     Scamander river, its bloody content

10   Questing when it appears in cubes?
     Quit my sight!
     The laughing voice was moved to
     Pity, more bitter than awful vane
     A bitter lesson upon their palate

15   Breath of nothingness, like clumsy mass,
     With sound of tempest, earthquakes,
     Fire and blood, I changed the bid
     The will of my throaty mutter
     Was a crying soul, caught in

20   The web of entangling mess
     I had luck with my heart
     Saved the panging soul
     Goodness of my heart answered
     Through heartiness and joy

25   I was left to pass

Easy – Round Way

As it came, 'twas right for them to say
Loo! Comrades boasting emptily
The pride of their joy
That was not right,

5. I spoke to them with brimful lashes
   Effect of which scorched me,
   Drugged or hypnotized or what, you would
   Never imagine ever
   Like frightened debtor, I waited to see

10. Rejected by all, including my good humourous talk,
    Someone is calling to see my face,
    'Twas sharp, just as it was clear
    Throbbing heart, beating, panging
    The impulse showed me the visible way

15 Jovial shudder waving with the rattle
   Spastic shake ending in coarseness
   Croaking voice beckoning for help
   Snaking there and there, all drew with pain
   As spittle of blood ran down the way

20 It joined the other side, vanishing into void
   Emotionless but much troubled
   What?
   I heard havoc! Evil being, leave us!
   But not heeding, utter destruction

25 Seemed inevitable

Tribute to Departed Friends

Ah! Fading story of life,
The deep inset of mortal departure
What with the disillusioned light,
Darkness fails with persistent weapon

5.   Beckoning to love, much with vain hope,
    It still shrieks off the horizon,
    Astute shadow falling on the azure horizon,
    Seems the next blanket of vapour,
    Thick smoky mist imperializing lighted world,

10   All with dangling story and unsurpassed wealth,
    Flamboyant flowing of opulence,
    Still swirling on agony's dogma,
    The hard pains of life, hard to swallow,
    Lively nature, tiring in overcoming

15   A clamping of metallic hammer,
    Vividness with great sorrow,
    Lay the pierced heart, dangling on
    Low, roaring flame,
    I cried for you, such harmattan tragedy.

20   All farewells to all the beloved,
    What hearkens deep, strikes hard,
    Throbbed, it panted, it quaked,
    Such great dwindling, of all my grievances,
    Driving low, low ...

25.   'Twas now a voided movement,
    My fate was not the least touched,
    The powers beyond mortal reaches,
    Ending the verses in floating oblivion

Destruction of Evil Forces

It's bravery indeed!
Wonderful way of treasure packing,
Spiritual knowledge surpasses,
The craving of unconscionable beings

5   Doom of hopelessness inevitable,
      Sharply contrasts vividly, alluring,
      The deed of "gampoth,"
      Glorious one, piercing the stillborn darkness.

10.   Full of uncertainties, creator of hope,
      Sharp stump of obstruction, rising across
      The windy path
      Alone, dark oblivion, sinister whispering,
      Owls letting off prophetic hooting

15   Immaculate heart walks past the scene,
      "Gampoth," demolisher of anarchy,
      Dazzling personality, acclaiming knowledge,
      Gazing, albeit, winding his way,
      Down, the thickets where witches gather.

20   Summoning all evil forces,
      Ready to strike, creating chaos,
      Leaving looted-wailings behind
      Evil nature striving for strife,
      Champion of champions, devil of devils

25   Wailing, crying, we dwell in you,
      Mocking dew, dewing on our brow,
      Wet blood rolling over head,
      All are gone, beseeching all
      Our path.

30   We take down long talons,
      Tooted monkeys unto the deep, flung,
      Abyss of demons – a grave cave,

Chink of coming light, laughing,
Bashing shadows, sky of revelation,
No parallel since the history of the business.

35 Empty handed, blank headed,
    Power washing away, leaving all in peace?
    Potali! Akoumin! Throaty cry,
    Sucked mouth's vomit, unheard yet,
    Gate of eternal wisdom opens, opens ...

40 Not for all,
    Begging, crying, enticing, enchanting,
    Knowledge vanishes away,
    Paradise of eternity flung open for them.

The Price of Recklessness

Grey dawn strikes the mortals,
The wave of foam washing away,
Angry roars of airy mouths, crying,
Interjection of immortalities

5   "Cramp it up,"argu'd men of underworld,
    Hope of crossing the Oxus sea
    Down to the mouth, gulping down,
    Inside the deep abode of Zambis,
    The flame of fire, rising high

10 Dogmatic vapour eating all,
    Still buried in the quaking sound,
    Attendants of numerous entities, hovering near,
    Waters of grave flourishing,
    Still rocketing the tempestuous season

15 Sailing, our men steadily move,
    Rising wind blowing hard,
    "Lathe" of darkness engulfing them,
    Re-awaking spirit parting before them,
    The voyage is done, doom

20 At hand.
    Flashing eyes, seeking preys,
    Angry, roaring, hoarse voices like
    Sediments of horror that boil down,
    Darkness of death allowing not

25 The besieged the use of the sea, land and air.
    When the rusty bomb pierced thru'
    All was consumed by beams of thick smoke,
    Washing sound, erupting gallantly,
    Demolishing, devastating, leaving nobody safe

30 Thousand Voices of commanding irrepressibly,
    Unaware beats the bravest
    Due preparation, a figure of bygone time,

Exposing the extremes of weakness,
With the balancing of trumpet's sound

35 Signal of triumph, all deserted,
Cold ashes of waste mingle with bony parts,
Alpine water, gathering deathless force,
Forcing – down-gloomily.

40 Inhabitants of dark world,
Was it a dream or a phantom,
Vigilance was lacking, evil doom
Not avoided

Unforgettable

Flood has carried away all the stalks,
Chance to recover, dying in hopeless gesture,
Not so the day
Gravely wounded lions chased all my people.

5   Deep, sharp edges of frozen hedges, rising approvingly.
     All the paths are blocked,
     Locked down to end for no good cause!
     Where I cling has broken off
     Branches of life, dangling loosely!

10 If you see them, no suffering exists, you will think,
     Obstinate desire lagging behind aimlessly,
     Bearers of death among the hidden thicket
     Unyielding, dominion of fair fairies

15 All are killing my glory!
     All have some, rhythm of dance,
     Vibrating to the feel of intense heat.
     Walking from where I came
     Not possible, running round the bend,

20 I came to an abrupt stop.
     There, Alas! Face to face with tip-tat fingers.
     Roaring, flaming fire issuing forth,
     A heart of steel inside,
     As vapours and mists cast a veil

25 'The underworlder' who devours
     Root of your life stays killed by me,
     See none, but look back quick,
     I know all, perished them,
     Shall then the curse be upon hapless souls?

30 Driven, strong to have,
     "So it's you that has done it," said I
     "Keep fit and continue thy work"
     But once gully erosion got hold of the earth,

I demand the compensation for it.

35 If not, full force shall come to react,
   It ends not there
   Talons – of long beasts
   Tranquil motion of impulses, descending
   Monotonously, xylophone of dance coming,

40 Vibrating, throng's of ghosts, of madness!
   Where was I?
   I was crowded, engulfed by forces of
   Dark world, where I can't rise,
   Dawn was smashed to fragments

45 Set-fold of joy pushed away,
   Only the merry dark was heard,
   From where none has ever gone,
   Arose the queen of ladies,
   A soloist of jazz singing serenely

50 Wait for it to come again,
   Yes, Ha! He! Hi! I went really mad
   Laughing with me!
   Was I sure it really came to pass?

55 Indeed, a great Indaba happened
   Follow, follow, come gaily,
   Down, deep shall hours pass,
   Pure bred flowers telling woeful
   Tales, queen mother listens not

60 Depth of water-grave,
   Child of many wings
   Spirit cursed – fellow, follow
   It down to the depth of fire
   Ha! He! Hi! They said.

65. Such experienced I, but still alive,
    My fate better than all I knew,
    They gave me hand to catch fly
    I knew what it was, a living legend,

Bathing water to escort me

70 Was that too late?
    Never shall I forget
    All my people are there, soundly
    'Twas drawn apart, ending verse,
    Closed

75 Nightmare of wonder,
    A long tale of narrative poetry,
    Lyric tale upon a savage blow,
    I lived apart, a secluded life

Ishirikpam

All lay still, vibrating,
Intense heat rises and falls,
Flashing eyes searching for
Ominous things

5.   Several insects, with much cunning,
    And uncaged,
    Millions of eerie sounds descending,
    Diminuendos from evil, immortal being,
    Suddenly it leap'd and tors'd.

10   Up high, sparks spurting,
    Head diving below, answers yet
    Fearful voices, sighing in
    Anguished silence,
    Way in, and way out, throng of eye

15   It went, barbarous plants,
    Powerless to quench "Ishiri" light,
    Cut sharp like glittering stump
    With considerable havoc, done

Down to Mortals

Rusty beings in earthly mood,
Rushing towards the dawn,
And loud with metallic force,
Alas! Not minding the rotten smell

5.   Mingling and plunging down
    When the shower was clear,
    But Alas! Upon and upon all life,
    Splitting along the windy path,
    Where life was shining

10   Inside, the influx of mortals
    Descended,
    Until the day their debt was paid

Goodness of the World

The land to live reveals good virtue,
What nature has in store, incredible!
With good hope, then,
Reigning and ushering in good speed

5. The distance of poor
    Life stood trembling and faint-hearted,
    Could it be time melting
    In tiny air?

10. The creator looked well and saved
    His people from the loss of indemnity

Beautiful Heavenly Paradise

Through the Almighty's ample sphere,
It went, revealing
Twenty torpedo images shaking,
The quake of baleful eyes,
Light of heavens, shining, shining

5.   Empty command, calling all to dwell,
    Water mingled with fire,
    Steeped with deep gaze
    As it sped, to return no more
    Blazing heights of valley and

10.   Mountainous rangers,
    Mammalians alive, bowed with intent.
    Through fancy spell, unseen,
    No dreadful spring night in sight,
    Blazing, vibrant, widely apart

15   Death to foaming waves as
    They clanged against the rocks,
    Deep – at the base of waterfall
    Together, all hurled with
    Physical sphere,

20   The Rocks and ocean were
    Swiftly, swirling,
    But they were not to see
    The heavenly palace that accommodated me
    As joyous laughter broke

25   Then, pregnant silence ...

Foolishness and its likely Repercussion

What among men is the blessed life?
To a few, godliness is somewhat
Known, failure of thought from
The "modicum" of sealed lips

5. The flame of life, thrown into air,
   Spirit of nature vanished with laughter
   Tell me, all ye that see
   Nature with its twinkles,
   The knowing was superbly done

10. As exposition strikes hellula!
    Like a senseless, jiggling witch,
    Promise of which acts like a
    Two –edged sword
    Hour of enjoyment, burdensome

15. The captivating veil of a shrouded reign,
    All bound to the wing of a compass,
    Beyond the whole lovely melody,
    Gone with terrible force,
    Roaring under wooden possessing

20 Inverse,
    But the over shadowing gloom
    Will not vanish
    Foaming sight over thine
    Azure dome, behind a besam tree

25 Withering light was no more seen

Rain

The alluring bow of brightness,
Arching grimly, dazzling piercingly,
Clearing away
Radiance of sorrow

5. Its striving point blurred by a new
Wave,
The golden, azure horizon deepened,
The gloomy wind blowing quickly,
Alas! Quaking voices of cloud,

10. Forces of blackness, inheritors of the dark,
It dropped down with mounting intensity,
Rocketing voyage of arrowing light,
Buried by the thick edge of blanketing
Cloud

15 A ringing glow flashed through innumerable slits
A voice of metallic influence, crying?
Boom! Sound vapouring, vapouring
Harshness of ash, slowing down,
Fierce brothers of dewdrops, fighting

20 Again the violent shaking, succumbing,
Subjugating, dwindling powers of lightning,
Hoarse streaks in sky's temple,
Loo! It came, sheets of coldness,
Flaming searchlights sending quivers in all direction

25 Bantum! Bambun! Every way it came,
Eternal gate of heaven flung open,
The rain of tears, weaving the dews,
Scattering, – enchanting, tempting kids

30 Cries of excited children running about,
Voices of mothers roaring through the darkness,
Being companion only by flashes and
Rumbling, accompanied by increased

35 Menace of flooding power
   Slumber unfurled with zeal,
   Pieces of cold ice breaking the
   Stillness, melting in rainy sand
   Or picked by curious children

40 Abruptly, resolution not yet subdued,
   A clear emotion pushing all,
   All the same it seemed to have actively
   Partaken of the patrol of windy water
   Suddenly, it comes propelling ... again ...

45 The nature ... the nature of rain water

Pushing the Bridge of Stone

Clamour of humorous melody,
Came buzzing like a swarm of bees,
Such groovy sight kill'd everybody
With happy minds

5   Chatting merrily o'er the low bar,
     The fence of morality, entrance
     To understanding
     'Twas like being thrown apart when
     Low musical instruments entered

10. If we ever waited to view our seas,
     All surging to acquaint themselves for the last,
     Noise of the cymbal,
     Clanging of the labyrinths
     Alas! Singing with holy trumpet!

15 Lyre over the grave fence
     Indeed, it was joyous, intoxicating,
     It came waiting in the air, throbbing,
     Zambezi-like music

20 It seemed not what we thought of,
     Nothing of the sort, as it looked,
     Utterance of delight,
     Gold-rimmed peasant's laughter
     A scorching sound, irritable

25 Such was the ghost of corrupt
     Forces of darkness, 'obeyers' of the devil,
     With my spluttering ship's – speed
     Borne to wonderland
     My hollow statute was saturated

30 Greetings of goodwill, better than
     Blossoming rosy flower,
     Still not contented, wanted badly
     To quench, and destroy again,

Ambitious doom awaits them

35 A threat from above makes
Them victims of wreckage,
If they disagree, let them try
And bear the reproach
Which nothing can throw away

40. Our ears are closed to their cry,
This I decree ... only I ...

Price of Immorality and Illegal Acquisition

Alas! The glory has departed
Hour of pasture buried in hideous myth
Vehemence of wisdom vanishing

5   Oppressors dominion marching
      Along the grassy path, woe!
      Oh tale, power of fruitlessness,
      The 'Lastaras' homecoming
      Galloping alone, fluttering winds

10   Thru' their dance, claiming all the
      Blood of lineage, descendants' ancestry,
      The material concerns dwindling
      All hope of pomp succumbing
      Material opulence coming home with a

15   Hopeless gesture
      It was thrown down, deep down, chained ...
      Abyss, breeders of monsters,
      Fierce confusion among the gathering,
      All waited for long, darkness falling,

20   Still no sign of its appearance
      A doomed bride, woe of woe,
      Glad to approach, all dusty feeling,
      Crying, throwing all forces aside,
      Selfish cause of survival not attained

25   Attribution, at least, lasted more than hours,
      Moaning coming from a tethered bull
      Conduit of water, gravely, he was
      Dragged, so continued the revenge of a
      Sinister world, shrill deepening darkness

30   It sprang with rocky chest,
      Lifeless ghosts surrounding me,
      Advancing, I cried, loo! A grave will,
      No period of thought, a silent

Time between the hour, and dawn passed,

35   Still, I was rooted to one point,
Only with cheerful vision did I survive
The woe
I cried, my eyes wet with tears
The vengeance is done

40   Noble demigods chatted for
No good, messy ground served
For its conveyance
Silence wilting, owl hooting tantalizingly

45   Here come I, standing among them, the
Fresh blood poured out of my people
Bumping heart, panging freely – no hope
It was 'thicket-dark', his blood was
Flowing, splinting, joining the bad

50   Ones,
Unseen ghosts crying, beckoning to
The dead periwinkles
All hovering among the showy
Scene, singing in monotones

55   Woe, woe, all falling forward,
Possessors of illegality, all joining
Together, bending, not leaving ...
Gatherers, go gladly, worldly, no
Chance for illegal cravers

60   It's done, wherefore they were gone,
To wit, price of immorality
Inevitable among the deathless ones
That saw the rock of evil
Shouting, rushing wildly, madly ...

Unshakable Rock

I

I was led away,
Over the cliff, deepening grey,
We crossed the rocky path,
Up through crags of thicket

5.   Jungle of mammalians, dwelling ground
     Of craziness, where charging bulls fight,
     Devouring and eating, the condition of
     Existence among the legendary world
     Sharps of stumps hovering over thine head

10   In ecstasy of agony,
     Deep pitched, wave of woe,
     Unnerving sound of thunder
     Near or far, I knew it was near,
     My friends - all my glory is gone,

15   All vanished metallically in the air,
     Gone by, the bygone days,
     When the flowers rotted,
     A house of merriment built under
     Shades of ripened *Ukwa* fruits,

20   What is that challenging my inheritance?
     All treasures dissolving like
     Heated sugar
     Easy to melt, if touched by grey,
     Listen …. I want the tale of woe told

25   Deeply, conscious of noise, absorbing,
     Declaring, ravishing, with boundless force,
     I cling to my right foot,
     A great blow passed
     Dark spurt of blood filling up …

30   Oh, what has wetted the dew?
       A fool, oh fool, holy blood of yours
       Falling like poor bent bow
       A sweat of hardship gulping down
       Sky born child, raging with my weeping

35   Left hard dangling loosely,
       Rumbling volcano, when will it stop?
       "Proceed, carrier of pleasure,
       Dainty spirit hovering about
       A warring servant of beauteous azure

40   Light, my severed hand obstinately stands
       A waning foot, striving to survive,
       It has finished, so ends the regale"

II

Intractable Element, Learned Philosopher

45   All done to me, still standing gallantly,
       Olden good days, when my valour was bred,
       Brandishing the golden sheild of
       Athena, much loved, I salute my heart,

50   It blossoms, blossoming, spreading
       Rock of stand, vanquisher of demons,
       All was done by me
       Touched by the mortal part

Voices of the Sea, Legend, Thunder

Roaring voices of jagged rocks,
Splint! And back to the
Sorrow land, by that time
It wasted much hope,

5.   Dark! By daring,'twas
    Never seen, a sizzling sound
    Crumbling, waves, torpedo-like
    Dash! Over the gloomy scene
    Far away, it was from a callous
    Hand

10 Queen mother laughed mirthlessly,
    Wait and look back to the
    Magnification of senses,
    Alas! With wrath guiding

15 Down, and with appalling strength,
    Flying across the
    Alley, where "Okepetu" was
    To be seen in the

Dead horizon where they dwell

20 Along the sloppy hills
    It vanished, with a flash
    Opening up, and lightning piercing,
    Throwing away shadows ...
    Delight, rumble! It went

25 And sounded with agility

Fox in Sheep's Skin

I

I am on a long journey
Crossing many wild lands
All leopards bowed for my passage
Lions stopped roaring before my power

5.   Trumpets of gizzards halted, my power again,
      Trunks of elephants hacked down
      We crossed many evil forests
      The land of ghosts and gobblins
      Kingdom of spirits,

10   When I looked back, my followers ran
      Away, I stood, alert to know the cause
      Below where the jungle thicket
      Started, a bellowing came,
      My hand was filled with oil

15   The oil that passed many yams,
      Rocketing sound of angry bulls stopped,
      Baying sound of giraffes quenched,
      Low moaning of rhinos, a mere nightmare,

20   The shadow of light
      Sunlit world shuddered away from my
      Grave power
      Flames of exhorted kisses
      Crying signs of wind, quiver of

25   Slippery water
      They had gone dead since,
      Horror of glory, long forgotten,
      Wind rustled, and whispered where I stood,
      Swaying trees, naked leaves dangling,

30   All the paths, and tracks, all covered,
      Envious eyes cast by the scrambling ones,

As my laugh echoed – re-echoing,
The blood of my enemies froze
But still far away they dwell,

35 Abode of darkening wood
Voices of song drifted by the wind
Settling rapidly, mingling with
Nature's grooviness, all delighting me

II

My long journey was still far away

40. Receding forces seemed to retreat,
Upon the steps of my feet
Anger rose
Dim waters of ebbing sea, cooling,
Elms of deep watery grave, alone,
Alone

45 I cast a shadowy eye among them
Even nymphs of olden days stopped running
I halted to know if the obstinate one was there,
No! Nay, only, the good ones all along,

50 They gave me grand leave
If I cut the calm sea
What will I see?
A fresh blood flowing,
The head of a monster

55. Laughing lips of mermaids
I stood, aloft, to decide my fate
All my power banged, panged and quaked,
I laughed again and descended twice

60 Towards the rising sun, it went,
Back blizzard horizon, where
They went along
The sloppy range
Fountains of pain,

65 Jungle of demons, they went
    I crossed the path, stepping on
    Blood,
    From my deep cut, they were issuing
    Rustle of wind again

70 Roar of lion near,
    Monsters from sea poised,
    I cast a long look and paused
    They all feared and gave me way,
    In my hand they dropped, rooted,

75 Beams
    My eyes narrowed, a greedy one,
    I knew it not that death itself,
    Ate, all in a twinkle,
    Curiosity kills

80 Further still beyond the sea,
    I climbed all mountains
    Stepping on messy earth,
    The woods sighed
    Nri dwarfs laughed,

85 Alone upon the anthills' abode,
    My finger was raised,
    The insult was too much to bear
    They scrambled to rise no more

III

I have reached the end

90 End of things never dies,
    Since million years – I continued to go
    But, now, where are the enemies?
    All had fled when they heard,
    Only ancestors of mine remained

95   I dwelt with them forever
      Beyond the beyond, crossing grassy paths,
      You can't see where I went
      The way is closed,

100 Be content with what you have
      The parted ones – full of honour
      Laugh as you like, but bear in your
      Deeper soul, never grow as I grow

Fools

Rise – high – higher,
Sound! Again spark,
Rent above the
High twilight world

5   Engulfed in the air, the dews
    Dream'd of what happened
    What had passed away
    Change mortality to immortality
    Cause of explosion of the mind

10 Fools! Why these throngs of
    Cry when the cause
    Was for paying one in one's own coins
    We heard the dinful roar
    From sleep to silence, the wailers,

15 Bad memory lay among them

Visible Power of Darkness and Light

Milky dusk, shining dimly down
Beautiful laughter, half-heartedly made,
Gathering its winding force, towards
The remission of its life's extracts

5   The shadow of life, the giver of light
      Among the demonic bondage,
      Your great power never succumbs,
      Striving happily, chirping merrily,

10 Azure golden horizon, gone,
      Millions of thy sparkle,
      Lifting up the gate of heaven
      Young pregnant beauty, surpassing
      All the dwellers of the hollow sky

15 Yours is the wonderment of
      Power, shower of light, dispenser
      Of sorrow,
      Scorning all, challenging all,
      Omnipotence of your power

20 The great one driving with words,
      Home, home, oh!
      Where they dwell among us

Captives

Low rumbling of uprooted stone,
Gazing steadily on its downward journey,
The mission of vengeance upon its voice

5   Quaking river god with ringing voice,
     Sorrowing sharply against my ear,
     Its monotonous laughter, kindred's spirit,
     Meeting cannot solve,
     Piercing high, shrieking higher, up-up-up

10   Among the gloomy, dark clouds
     All sat quiet, cowed completely
     Clambering along the elms, eroded with
     Mighty force
     Metallic talon-like throat, gulping the bitter liquid,

15   War of vengeance seems different now,
     Gangling! Clapping! Welcoming -
     Beckoning flocks to see the
     Captives, low eaves together,
     Lurking sleepily like rams of

20   Sacrifice
     Again it sounded,
     Long jaggered rock
     Splinting down, raising void in
     Space, blank with blind

25   Oblivious dark, violence of nightmare ...

Indemnity of Hell

A great unjust one facing a just one
Shrieking, quivering
With tumult, no remedies
Alas, my application for restitution, denied

5. Appeal to higher justice, was
   A dreamland vision
   Oh- lo! The final case
   Settlement was close at hand
   The judgement will be fierce soon

10. The horror and terror weigh you down
    But when human emotions lead,
    Seeing is impossible
    Bowed head, clinging brow,
    Jerking hand as black as shadow

15. Lead you unto the realm of
    The darkest immortals
    No remembrance, nay forgiveness,
    The sinful unquenchable fire,
    Flies away, mystical chain

20. Seems like chronic song of
    Black sinners, thy companion in the
    Land henceforth!
    Lucifer's message echoed to you

25. "We drive thee to our
    Bunker, high rose
    Powerful men, join us
    To inherit the unseemly
    Land and dwell there
    To live as us

30. Is there any other punishment
    Greater than dwelling in a lion's den?
    Life of fire, burning dazzlingly

Oh, how terrible
Paying for immoralities – iniquity of sin

Debt of Sorrow

I dived into it - deep
Never knowing what lay
In store for the ignorant one
The little creeping scene had vanished,

5   Replaced by a more undesirable one,
What's the nature of this?
Life led by the dying was
Dangerous, also for the sufferers,
But Alas! I stopped there,

10   No human will left
Come to my sight and be on
Guard after finding your way
What is it for now? When the
Sun had refused to arrow down

15   Its rays towards me,
The moon! Blood stricken,
With jagged layers of bitten brew
Wave of water beating all
Around, while spirits

20   And 'underworlders' pursue the poor ones
High streaks of lightning coming
Down and descending with metallic force,
Deep rumbling accompanying them

25   Incredulous outlook,
It was wonderment again
Through the vale, with blooming
Inlay,
Calling thousand flowers

30   Strayed far from life,
Longing mortals' life alight,
My voice croaked, hardened,
And looked on in ecstasy of violence

Power of hate, the energy of life
35 Give me, oh give me,
Give me the miracle of joy

Great Ancestors

Departed ones, I salute you,
Great ones that know ominous' morrow
Let us not down
Our cries, lamentation croaking with

5   Throaty voices,
     Implore you
     Remember us great ones!
     As we invoke the greasy grey
     Ground that split over there at

10   The grave side, to be the
     Good son to you
     Beautiful, fearless ones
     Protect us from ill wishes
     Bellyache, headache,

15   Mouth swelling and throat sore,
     Disillusionment vanishes because
     Of your presence
     Vituperation and evil tribulation
     Depart as we sing thy praise

20   Great ancestors, impartial judges,
     Guide us in our undertakings
     Insert brilliant light and
     Judge as you do when
     Lizards approached first, their early coming ...

25   Seeing that you let us not down,
     Your breeding youth ...

Obstinate Pones

Mighty pones, the end goal is near,
Near death wish craving, closing
Verses of love, vision of nightmare

5   All between the valley of frosting forests
      Night's long journey, striving to go
      Between you, a river of flowing
      Blood, messy vultures hovering near,

10   Drink deep! Oh glorious twilight
      Grey passage of light hidden by
      Boulders
      Foaming water, where to satisfy your thirst,
      Don't shudder, keep fit and go

15   Before the spread feet of
      Terrible avengers
      Hapless creature in misery, waiting for
      Your fiendish eyes of glowing mist,
      Death to put an end to sorrow instantly

20   Alas! No, nay, I to throw them down
      Slate of despair, evil bigger than ever,
      Expands
      Reversing horrified movement
      A splint, look back along the alley

25   Deep smoke has risen,
      So great its depth I cannot know
      Dragons, raving, ravaging, devastating
      Drink deep, oh poor wretched soul,

30   I leave you there, such a waste
      An obstinate one tackling endless fiascos,
      So fade you, great one
      The parting was brutal, I can't do much
      Leave them there, worthless spirit

35 My rolling malignant rage against
    Recklessness of thou
    Stands alert, a wave has come,
    Shadow of doom covering the cloud
    Glorious pones, so ends your life

40 How are the brave fallen
    Power to fight dwindling,
    Back and forth, the smelling continues
    Hither comes the boar, angry flashes,
    Blood of demon, avengers of blood,

45 Up and down I gaze with frightful eyes,
    Such time when needless, hopeless thought patrols
    Ancient of doom, receiver of attack

50 Summoners of unwanted powers,
    The great pones have gone,
    Child of river birth, blood of the
    Royal prince, mingled with
    Worthless 'watery' grave,

55 Blood of great man, so
    Uselessly used
    I fainted down, awaking at dawn,

Trapped

I was bound with throngs of iron,
Faltered with hovering cloak of
Night, the veil of prevalence, still lurking deep, deep

5   They threw me into it to die,
    But the shining radiance struck
    At my cloth,
    'Twas a great astounding fight,
    Flapping from the wages of sorrow

10 Escaping away through lonely
    Channel, I drank there, the water
    of the pond,
    Greyish taste that kept me shrieking,
    Running down, deep into the alley.

15 All looked on,
    I was running sloppily, covered with
    Mystic lowering, drowning with
    Showering forces,
    I was caught in the web

20 Of darkness, red arrows of
    Your arrogance, why not reach me?
    The bloodiness of Hades,
    Spirits waiting attentively to devour,
    Each tired, springing away,

25 But not embracing the sorrowful one,
    Each time melting into tiny air,
    And alone, what pleasures have I?
    All the gazing has effect upon me,
    What causes my young blood to

30 Spittle away, like a generous mess of soil mucus,
    The worthless markers are laughing
    Now, thinking that all is over,
    I took deep a breath, crying aloud

35 All gathered to hear my myth,
    What great legend it turned out to be
    Again it melted them, dissolved and
    Softened their hearts,
    Swallowed me up and caused
40 Immortal fame to rest in my persistent glory

Caricature Sickness

Don't shout the omnipotent name,
Purring of the heart with
Throbbing sound
5   Tells you what to do,
    You did, you discern abnormality,
    Listen to the little verse that
    Shook their wavering fate
    Alas, spirits of light and dawn
10 Lifting up the oceanic water
    They dispense profanity, name of the evil eye
    Corpses of infected beings laughing monotonously
    Let go of the dazzling darkness
    Full of waxing boulders, clear not your
15 Mind
    Again, see it coming with tormenting
    Speed, hear it boom, sending your
    Talks asunder, see it coming, scattering your
    Vows, sending you into the abyss of mother – earth,
20 Smell it well to end thy sun
    Alas, we are all back
    Singing mirthlessly
    We give glory to all
25 The good helpers to live,
    Out went the waves,
    To replace the weakening
    Sigh for the better, because
    They needed a laugh
30 See, to live and forget all that,
    Better than not see the fading
    Of glory, the fate of
    A dead child born yesterday blooms
    More, spreading like a rosy bed of flowers

Impossible Trial

It echoes near, near
I say it sounds,
A wound curling around my power

5   It booms, calling all to listen,
      Hysterical gaze belongs to "Elonyato"
      It shook its root, laughing,
      Wickedly, by breaking the scene
      Horrible to behold

10 I saw it fall, lying among the groves
      It bit its root, soon pausing
      Well, look on and see what is there to see
      I fell away, buried deep with
      Thorns, I rose from beneath, stretching

15 Myself,
      When I stood up
      What met my gaze?
      Round ring of sorrow creeping
      Back again,

20 See me frown, wanting my prey,
      I don't know what seized my arm
      Fighting with weird creatures,
      Butting and striking to end my
      Lineage, I shook off

25 Sweat clearing from my brow,
      Oh, wound and the blood spilling out,
      Beyond! Horror! Cries of the poor
      Like countless sands of the seashore,
      All waiting to arrest my generation

30 They hope in vain to see my ruin

Sacrificial Sheep

With bounding powerful energy
All bleating well to swallow fodder,
Good of meat and pyre funeral
See you locked in gloomy pen,

5   Jerking your heads, striking thy fellows
     I know you all, foolish prey,
     Why are they always crying?
     Alas, the fate of the little ones,

10   The brain of your heads, worthless
     Or what, react! And hover
     Around, singing your sorrow,
     With metallic force that frightens
     Your eyes, they lead you on

15   Over the slopes, to graze no more,
     Down the plain, to scorn your life
     Deep spurt, hurtling down
     Closing verse – no more weeping
     The wail from your eyes only

20   Watery tears to fall on the lonely ground,
     Under the groove of Amadioha
     There you lay, to say yes
     Alas! For whom, cruel existence

25   Why do you not want to see any more
     Sunshine? your fate is wearing out,
     Altering, falling to pieces
     Front of thy wide lung to
     Tear in fragment,

30   In fact the cruelty is hidden
     When you cringe, with choking
     Force thy blood spurted along
     Inside the basin, there to stay
     Until when the world resolves that

35   You do your part

Hopeless Whited Sepulchre

Adamma of "Ogirish" branch,
The shining rose with hollow mole,
What withholds thy grace?
Causing your beauty to mingle about

5   Your uprising seems delicious
    Towards me,
    Young supple grace, protruding intrudingly,
    The dignified movement raising applause,
    Solid "boulder" descending tantalizingly

10 Raw, naked, natural arch advancing high,
    Under the sweet laughter beckoning
    Bachelors
    Glorious movement mounting in ecstatic
    Mound,

15 Alas! The bashing veil
    Drifting away
    Reveals the emptiness of hollow world
    Of power shrieking towards the
    Womb of the unknown

20 Affecting not the hearts of
    Immortal depth
    Scornfully, smiling messily away
    No! Rain of sorrow,
    Working less with the dewy tears

25 Falling
    The great work of sensibility
    Dwindling among the hovering air

The Coming of Riverine Flocks

Upon the grove of immortal fame,
Come upon the world with unhindered speed
Away thru' washing blood
Of Sytr's bulky bank

5   Rippling, heaving, quaking the roots
      Of oceanic source,
      Upon the waters deepening down,
      Alas! baffled gaze stupefied by terror
      And frozen horror

10   They are stupefied, again, again
      Among the growing
      Mast of shredded glory
      Folding joy and peace
      Come what looks like

15   Blood laughing, smiling,
      Mysteriously languishing, shrieking, vanishing –
      Gulping down the fierce
      Savage power of supernatural force
      Accompanying a raving fiend,

20   Deep rumble spreading after,
      The wonder striking, violently shaking,
      With burning, bloodied heart,
      Approaching the habitants
      Of mortal world

25   Welcome home, a riverine flock of 'Olu'
      That's the grandees ushering the
      Golden, black blood
      Of pure incorruptible race,
      Ancestral fathers dwelling

30   In the bowels of watery graves,
      Waiting patiently for their turn, to
      Join and form the long line
      Of a marching race ...

Lack of Understanding

Wide awake but dead
Mortally,
What nature has in stock for them,
Yelling and snapping closely,

5   The 'yeye' that wanders far,
      To see the harder part inside, and
      Worked harder, secret of
      My strength has been respected
      Owing to the vanishing mirage

10   They maketh themselves
      Sightless to the power
      Before them, afar, but near ...

Away with the Contented Heart

Splashing and flapping noise,
Chuckling,
Away to gold mine
Down the alley it descends

5   Kissing waves blocking companionship,
     With all my knowledge and power
     Feet with cold shuddering fever
     Stand on my way stubbornly
      Obstinate and intractable essence

10   Vacate my sight and quit thee!
     Far gone! Alone on the path
     That leads up to where I come,
     Disappearing with satisfied heart

Suffer my People Naught

Retribution swallowing up
The evil done
What seems down refuse to go,
Plunging deep to the inner part,

5   Clothed with thorn, horror seeking all,
    Like insane lion to devour,
    What it is up to
    I cannot tell,
    But see them crowding

10 Lurking from the edges
    Of the bank, to gaze no more,
    It all hurtled to many parts
    Calming others to go down
    Fierce eyes controlling

15 Powers of darkness,
    Searching for sounds and letting them go
    Alas! What cause beckons
    That you have to do it?

20 What nature prevents them to see the dawn?
    All shrouded with myth,
    Enveloping mysterious outlook,
    To dwell among the sharp outcrops,
    How! It's done! What causes the

25 Sniveling, accursed be the
    Satisfaction of numerous wants,
    Receding, and buried in the
    Pages of ages
    Control it not, for the living dwell in goodness

30 When they see ahead, all wailing to strike
    As they move back through throngs of devils,
    Am I the one to stay and die shamelessly?
    Poor soul, let the curse
    Be upon them,

35 You have done naught, but sacrifice,
   Your royal blood, prey to jawless beasts
   What is that crying for?
   Like an unexplained mechanism,
   Drifting away, not knowing the children,

40 Where have they all gone?
   Dying for freedom, Alas!
   Am I still breathing?
   To hear the ominous wail,
   Gallant sons of God, you

45 Fought for your cause,
   Loo! Save them without
   Kindling the fire, loo!
   Still the blackness prevails
   The power of gloom and principalities

50 Laughing coarsely, mocking
   With madness, worry not
   When the cause be alternated,
   What have you done?
   Nothing, to see that equality reigns

55 They have gone bewilderingly aloud
   See them selling all their worth
   Away! They are driven from
   Their father's land,
   Where are they to go, then?

60 I cannot tell,
   Heartless, shameless beings!'
   Incredulous, ruthlessness
   How can I believe?
   Who will believe they can do

65 That
   All gone with nature's unification
   Now, their fame and
   Glory are broken in war

Land of Pleasure

We have arrived,
Direct into the mouth of pleasure
Clipping things waved us by
Mammalians singing choruses

5   To welcome us all,
      What is the nature of their song?
      It is dripping, wavering but loud,
      It evokes the merriment of life
      Echoing into the last unenclosed track

10   We all stood still capturing their voice,
      Which spread aloud, in rhythmic cadences,
      Beautiful ones, all laughing with
      Heart

15   Loo! Loo! Alas! Alas!
      Ringing us to pass,
      Unknown, but their
      Look pleases the eye

20   I have known that,
      I can still remember,
      Closing my eyes
      It came again, rolling in the wind,
      Throbbing in the leaves
      Bringing with it happy excitement

25   All waited, rending the windy air,
      O'er the track, down the 'alley
      Land of pleasure, what surpasses it,
      All fairing well, nurtured with gleaming looks
      What sort of paradise passes by us?

30   Many drinks to wine on
      Hovering over all the land
      Fishing pond, other objects to come,
      Surprised our shadows

           To the topmost peak

35   I don't know how to
     Express my thanks or what I say,
     Receding again, buried in the dim past
     Almost turning into legend, buried by age
     But fresh outlook, less of the tale,

40   Loving people who we can't pay
     Goodness moves us to show our joy,
     Laugh aloud! The sun
     Arises before mortals,
     Raining hard to enclose the wild

45   Die like a man and reign
     With steady soul,
     Goodness of heart,
     Much like the room of life
     Now we must look

50   With pulsing pulse

Long — Throaty Vultures

All was ready to go,
As if the deed was final
Indeed it was, doubtless,
Raised basins and cauldrons

5   And hollow containers
Until little spittle was
Rained down
Spluttering into the innermost depth
Of all the beings who were

10   Ready, but hovering above,
Covering the broad, blue sky
Like swarm of pestilence,
Flying beasts, much prepared
To do harm,

15   They descend down, to laugh
Like others long-throated too,
With sharp eyes picking
The wasted entrails,
Scattered, and away, all sounding

20   In unison of great song,
Perching among the branches of
Undulating palms,
Listening and looking down
To laugh some more

25   A game of mess, no matter
What obstructs the law of the land

Worthlessness

Down the busy street
All rushed past, the
Buzzing and buzzing
Alike, pushing up the mood,

5   Among the mass of
     Disappearing verses,
     Looking down the crowded world,
     Seeing the activities of nature
     To the dislikeness

10   Of the creator,
     Craving for earthly satisfaction
     Reasoning, not with heart
     But for satisfaction's sake
     Even with their life in quandary

15   Wild sins must be paid for
     Down corruption street
     Where bustle and hustle whistled by
     Fornication, devils, harlots, all alike,
     Corruption reigns with the wave

20   Of hopelessness
     Until it was well done
     That they lived alright, alright

Crushed To Pieces

A ghastly scene of horror,
Vision of nightmarish terror,
Such thick pack of human flow
The vein of wisdom, kingdom of hope

5   Such sight unalterable, along
      Rocky path, sprawling thoroughfare,
      Deep glow of rattling coming,
      Humid thicket of smoky smell
      Endless rusting to spasmodic shudder

10 Upon the blend, poor breed of
      Elegance
      Rolling along grassy side
      To avoid going down with
      Wilting, misty force

15 Voices of woe ringing out for
      Safety, it descends, crushing all to
      Pieces
      Upon the chattering, cowering
      Human soul

20 There lay it, wretched of mankind
      Manipulator of production
      Devourer of sleep
      The cruel rule of life
      Element of unhappy belonging

25 All waved aside, dark clouds
      Grimly, steadily and obstinately
      Patrolling, spreading, engulfing
      Favoured terror, deferred to death
      Compressed passion to draw near,

30 Crying,
      All together, hallowing the 'pully stark'
      Sublime of live

       Since last passed
       Lay upon the crowd, their brains

35   A messy look
       Penetrating hands, hurtling like
       Menelaus' shooting spear upon
       The golden shield of Paris
       It was done, vultures hovering

40   Trying to taste the waste of mortality
       Since hope of survival
       Dwindles away, only
       The immortals endure nightmares ...

Obedient Little Blush

My little flowering blush,
From your gleaming looks,
The spurt of your joy
Was great, much great

5   Pleased with my tete – a - tete,
      I danced all day to see
      My bloomy companions,
      Trotting along the steep
      Bank, wagging along ...

10   The disturbance has vanished,
      You see that which deserves to be good
      To swallow down the pleasing throat
      You loved me, why cant
      You respond? I say, why can't you respond?

15   Terribly yes, a million times,
      All entrails gulped down from
      Your mouth to your belly!
      Labour of work
      Laugh at me long enough if you wish!

20   I admire you well
      Feed your meat
      The better meat may
      Be sought in vain
      Sign of my devotion

25   Thicker than blood, your
      Heart joyful to see me

Too Strong to Punish

Slow, fierce wind appeared,
Ripped the face of humanity,
Long, washed white shadows
5   Of lights, varying,
    Blazing with constant velocity
    Vanished with them, went the thunder,
    On an internal journey,
    Suddenly, pregnant moon
10 Chases away the vapour of
    Insanity
    Instant judgment upon the clan,
    Gathering of gleaming shadows fled
    Black brow of anger
15 Patrolling the scenes on
    Sharp plains
    Jingles of mystic "Orism"
    Vacating the cluttered way to death
    Vengeance and destruction trying
20 To take who?
    Not I, a great child of many
    Worlds, let them search for
    Whom to devour
    A righteous man, light footed, with
25 Blank hope, the type to be preyed upon,
    Let the striving towards me fail
    A great Ukwa has fallen there,
    Away from the hearth as before,
    Beside it, flowing blood rose up
30 Dreamers for peace froze to
    Melting point, foolhardily rooted
    To a shaky path
    The way was open for them

Was I not covered by the

35 Hand protecting a succeeding reality?
But alas, fore here lay
The fence taking all in an embrace
The song was like a herb burnt nail,
Leaving a pastime of

40 Dreamland
Mirthless laughter shrieks
So low
From my revengeful heart
Where they stood, waiting for the

45 Worse, I cursed them again, they and the
Evil forces let loose by prowling bears,
Unknown, they have changed to stone

50 A store that remained there
When I grew,
We stepped on it,
A cool breeze always,
But the effect of danger was

55 Removed from our space

Salvation of Mortals

From the depth of heart,
Within the bowels of great power
Beneath the growing vale,
Washing away the mess of

5   Sorrow, but restitution acts,
    That which flows along,
    Running along where I could not step into,
    But not end it there, not there ...

10 Rolling over the road,
    Descending upon the winding path
    The low vision was grey
    Mess of dwelling abyss
    Until the mortals survive

15 To die no more
    It seems like a torpedo shake,
    Sending me to the realms of the unknown
    But retribution worked well
    Utter destruction avoided

20 Mortality then changed
    For a better cause

Peril in Dreamland

With a throbbing heart and panting pulse,
I ran into it
Not minding
what the cause will look like

5   Thrice I changed into "you and I,"
But each seeing nothing,
Only bemused,
The watery gaze vanished into
The air, 'chip, chip', pouring near

10   Save me with your power
See their coming, filing
With bombing speed, nuclear explosion,
Brandishing iron spear that
Thrust hard, down to the bowels

15   Of your being
Again, I went into it
Head swelling, hand quivering,
Legs no longer could carry me
Bending low until

20   I kissed the sandy foot,
Imploring, begging, enchanting,
Enticing, beckoning, hoping
For mortals' conscience sake, a release ...
One swift move, I was there,

25   Carried by them
A languid sigh of relief
When dazzling sun anoints its
Rays, my eyes opened and
Blinked joyfully

30   The bean was there
Directing the sun's arrows
Alas, it all came when Aurora

Of morning dawn sent her shadow
To spy the world

35 Dew of dangerous world vanished away
Morning glory settled, the blazing sun
Came, throbbing on the leaves,
In my deep somber state
I shook in fits and starts

40 All around me, I focused on nothing
Slowly, silently, then swiftly
I recollected the event and
Let out a hooting, throaty moan

Vengeance is mine

Floating raft sailing on shallow surf,
Down, between two golden moles it stuck,
Up towards the mouth of water flow,
Along the dark, steep alley

5   Gorgeous crossing between sharp stumps
     Dancing gracefully, beautifully,
     An abrupt gaze tells what awaits 'em
     Plight of morrow's
     Strand of air, engulfing ...

10   So, who knows the whereabout of the water beings?
     Dark trenches of hollow outlook
     A shining, dangling, dark hair
     An oval face, exposed raw beauty
     Smell of mound pointed towards

15   The direction of 'Hirikiri' side
     Long forgotten lake washed away,
     Farewell speech, a mere gesture,
     Stupefied steadiness, a forcing eye
     It bounds, moving, drifting

20   Over the winding grove, a scene
     Of humour
     All day long, a solitary watcher
     Feeding the salt sea, eyes, body
     Stood confused,

25   Alas, the people from 'Wakan'
     Long distant journey towards
     The western banks
     Across the slippery slope
     The wave, quaking, Anthill

30   Dwellers have risen
     An Olu descendant among the

Gruesome crowd,
Tiny sparkle at night to reveal
What they see, crags and all,

35 Whether intolerable, they spread,
Choosing boughs to refresh their being
A banging, full of horror
Seizure of innocent watcher
His manhood will be retaken,

40 Given away to rest, bargain for peace,
Oh it continued like a dark forge of fire
A risen lake, smoking gallantly,
Coils, seeking me out now,
Settling dispute among the elderly ones,

45 How insistent, hours of soothsayers
To conclude fast, for the sounding trumpet is
Descending again
Shall the rest of them fire back?
Cymbals of sound began, yet again

50 Rendezvous of rhythm plunging to eternity
Frenzily with murderous gaze, fierce hooting,
Up it raised the glittering hammer,
Rocks of vengeance, spy shall suffer
Dazzling shadows of dews still heaving

55 But lo! lo! It struck, ever shall it fall
Bringing down evil, necromancy needed,
Again he came to fulfill what
Was left

60 Showers of life are somber but greater,
Among the valley rising,
Gods of watery grave
Unknowable, enigmatic, silent ...
Wait for the price on your head

65 Devourer, a life shall never
Rest, singing the shallow hymn

Upon the rock of demons
Cheering away, shifting noiselessly
Thy people suffer, evil reigns!
70 A whole bull slaughtered to
Appease the immortals,
Come and descend o'er the gloomy barn
 Down
  Great waves heard it, a nodding in

75 Agreement, for the settlers will hurl
Volcanoes of bombs and rocks
With jagged
Catastrophic reverence, a striking
Force,

80 Ashes were setting down, pouring
Upon souls stretched lifeless,
Fingers of dreams ready to work
Was it all done to end?
The tale will never end, justice must

85 Be done

II

Emblems and shapes of spirits hovering over
Temples, alternating angrily,
Depart among an accursed one,
Light from venging sun coming

90 Forth
Foggy cloud and damp air heaving
Eros of rounded mouth
A hissing viper
"Come and take, eat to your full"

95 One by one, the earth fled,
Stung, deserted land in want of
Inhabitants
Was it the end to life?

Reincarnation was signed for those
100 Who wish to run
Happy life for workers of goodness

"Aerodim" (Plane)

Grand form of swirling
Whirling and tossing high
Up the broad heavenly
Sky

5   Lapping tossing mingling
    With the rumbling sound
    Deep like rumbling drums
    The nature of what to expect
    Like risen fire waves

10 Aims and scatters, far and wide
    Worldly beautiful creatures
    Moom! Room! GBAM! It sounded
    And with flapping wings like
    An aggressive falcon darting

15 After a prey
    It went, metallic 'allum' causing
    Much anxiety until
    It disappeared in the horizon
    Clothed with the browning

20 Hue of capricious rustiness
    The mission of vengeance is done

Departed Ones, Great Judges

I

The mess, so people thought,
A willow shark never falls down,
To be engulfed in the grim terror of a bad omen,
Now wait and hear the words

5   All came echoing through the dark night,
      First, it seems to be mingled with sweet
      Watery dew
      Darkness after dawn, a vision of horror
      O'er the bumping fence it descends

10   Full tragedy of it made known to them,
      Oblivion, the void of yawning
      Space notwithstanding,
      It came again, penetrating ...
      A chance once more, blackness returns,

15   Hurry, wait to live a happy life,
      But intractable vengeance holds sway
      To come upon them like fighting frogs
      Low moan of disagreement came
      Whirling along steep bank

20   O'er hedges of wonderment
      Entangling the masses of dunes
      Mass judgment of cold power
      Inheritors of great wisdom
      Helpers of mankind

25   Mountain beings drifted by,
      Birds whispered to let them pass,
      Clamouring, fluttering, with bowed heads
      Smoke rising from cold frozen
      Blizzards

30   Down o'er the west, it went,
       Clouds of simmering fire, burning low
       As it goes, all joined to one,
       Consuming agents of darkness
       Lightning flashes to acclaim the great ones

35   Snows melted, to form flowing water,
       To settle upon the jagged rocks
       'Elium' and other bowing beasts,
       Again, they came to land at the
       Clearing where all were sent to

40   Launder their pay

II

       Roar of applause, thunderbolt of joy,
       Sense of belonging, bumping hearts,
       Oh, pang of the grieving ones, settled
       To hear

45   Quaking, a violent shake, power
       Was there, long jump, drawn skirts
       Of wise ways
       Where the outcrop stumps,
       Roses of bedding plain, waters of Ngene River

50   All through the purification rites,
       It began, noises, voices of two sides,
       Wait! Hei! Stop to hear the row,
       Satisfied with what it says
       Yes, brow full of sorrow

55   Defame, what say you
       Alas! Upon the gloomy day
       Repentance was well done, horror
       Of bygone happy wishes
       Restless urge burning within

60   Hearts torn by grievous hand,
       Mind, soul, broken to pieces,

But await a bleeding
Wound to end its flow
So it shall be done to

65 Repair the rotten parts .
Hear the full content of judgment
Grinning, turning to easy laughter
Songs of "we shall not fail"
So be it, words of old true wisdom

70 Hearty congratulations exchanged,
All gone to happy sleep
Hearts cheering the great ones,
Seeking, acquiring their wisdom
Ancestors of masky threads

75 Indeed great, settlers of fraud

III

Buried with age, long forgotten,
Up and down, the world rolls
It soon shall come to light
When brutes came, did it start?

80 Ohoo! exploiters of economy,
Not then did we know,
Judgment of the good, 'bribeless' ones
Ever, ever ....
Not now, then, when they appeared

85 Subjugators did we know,
Hearty congrats turning into legend
Twist of life shall bring it to light
To know that our ancients
Deal more with problems than

90 Worthless parasites, only the
Pantheon of our dead reigned
When we were like a child, blind to evil
Some seek to deceive the golden pure blood of

Africans residing on ancestral lands
95 They know now, only now
And are torn, scramblers without shame!

Shining Moon – Daughter of Heaven

Beginning ...
The moon has risen
Seen in the middle, azure sky
Watched by curious eyes of kids
The watery world was devouring

5.   'Ubankwos' western world, glistening ...
    The shadows are heavy, calling,
    Calling the forest where water-birds dwell
    The moon has sharpened the way

10 Cleared the path of mortals' way,
    Gleaming down with wonderful
    Showering, the rays are hot, striking with intensity,
    To know if we shall receive them,
    The stars are appearing,
    Glittering among the traces of gloom

15 They are with the moon and sun
    Sweeping the Ilo where we play
    The shadow was coming - beckoning the moon
    He saw the moon and went to it,
    The path was clear, dazzling and wary

20 The road is clear by heaven's power
    The layout of immortal sources, showing
    The way we will take
    We will take to reach our destination

I

What led to the long journey,
Of hearing about Olane's vanishing
Melting like oil in the sacred mountain
Where he dwells, watching the pasture

5. Keeping the flocks of 'Alieoves'
Girth, Snow-warmed blizzards his
Companion, shaming the hope of the future,
That is on top like resting monkeys
Laughing scornfully at the dwarfs below

10 Listening to the eerie song of an epic hero
How he ascended to the throne of truth
And lost the mantle of his masters,
Judgment striking wildly into the forests
Of vengeance

II

15 How to know when it occurred
'Twas part of the hour of madness,
The blowing flames are scorching,
Chorus and song dwindling in hazy mirth
That was the time they set out

20 Along the edge of the frenzy land
Pastures of green world meadows
Crowded clusters of thickets
We journeyed in our bid to see
The pasture, and a bathing water source

25 Tongue of dragon, oh hungry wanderer,
Down upon rocky mounds
Monkeys chatter, birds clamour, wicked
Owls letting out their ominous hooting
We saw the play on jagged rocks

30 Thumping away the glimpse of a new shadow
The nude lips, laughing at the shadow,
Slowly, like butterfly noise, glided by,
Succumbing woefully into the ferns below

35 Over the foam of the god's water,
We saw the congregation, of
Reeds, calling the passersby to see for

Themselves,
Not for thee! Accursed be it,
40 Not for you! Our journey must progress
Even, when regal, with the law of nature,
So, we advanced far, far into the
Valley of Olum called the Pasture's abode

III

Wind rustled past in a mad frenzy

45 Apes walked upright, throwing rocks
With fiendish dexterity at the new sight,
Upon bones out of scourge, humans we are,
Trampled on, crippled by the misting time,
In Olum's world, the waster of fountain,

50 Of the ranges of Ida, where they met,
Of nymphs growing, springing up, enjoying
the dreamy haze
It was not that, the story of nightmare,
Fantasy, but we saw 'Dienings' and

55 His immortal, deathless – perpetual pasture.

IV

It was
Where they sleep, we know of it
Back, back, for the time expires
The sun is disappearing again,
The moon is approaching the
Horizon, turn and travel back along
The narrow path
What was he saying?
Dazed, stunned and daunted, dwelling on lost
Memories: It came, as if washed ashore with

65 Sharpened edge, raised over the broad

Back, a female sickle that spurts
Uranus' golden blue blood, brandished,
By Olum's demon to inflict
Uneven pain, like paralyzing hopes,

70 Clawing to see the sunshine of morrow
Lo! It waxed, and strangled ...
Over the plain, plunging into
Yawning abyss, where even the
Erinyes, Hicaroans and crossed -

75 Eyed, huge trunked cyclops abode,
We saw the goal and knew that the
Old and new, time past tide,
Are good

1   Up, over the Zeus skies,
Around the thicket of immortal crest,
Where the water birds clamour
Daring the searchlight of the heaven

5   Born.
Blow the waning fire,
Down upon the watery sea,
Peering dimly through the awakening sun
Seeking beyond but, lo, beyond mortals

10 Heard Aphrodite there, clung to by Ares,
To relax over the triumphant
Nations
Spirits have all vanished into void
Fluttering older beings in meta-creation

15 Gone into 'aboding' Hades of Poseidon
Mingling with low elms for easy pleasure
Undaunted, an obstinate heart stood,
Quenching deathless waves of winter storm
To save the innocent heart that

20 Dwells not long after,
The path is narrow, jagged and cracked,

The thunderbolt is booming, raking away
Monkeys! Clowns! Clatter back,
Standing by to see my beloved partner

25 Your love, eternal in the dim of
Creation, who to leave a spirit
Burning there of rust, nor glorious
Depth of heart, where the Ichor's nectar flows,

30 Pledge by a stirring, vaulting soul, leaping
That unquestionable bird, grips,
Draws, draws away to the shining paradise ...

Book of Dislocation

Mystery of Disappearance – Blown up

From where it came, alarming
Force of nature, blasting through window
Screens, drifting, swaying living things
What accompanies it, like rage of currents

5   Banging, clanging wooden doors
     Everywhere, rushes past, pushing,
     Afraid of the mad wind
     Suddenly, all lay quiet, panting
     After the march of buzzing sounds

10 Littered leaves, rusty hinges, flying
     Recklessly, fluttering in the void of space
     Again it rose, fiercer, electrifying,
     Blindingly raising sands in the tiny air,
     Under many covers it went

15 To strike, trying hard to deprive,
     Loo, crumpling noise filling the
     Open frontage from tens of feet,
     Down it went to the unknown
     Many are gathered, others lost,

20 Anxiety and excitement intermingled
     Desiring not to see if they are complete,
     Pouring down in full glory
     Through tiny sparks, penetrating,
     Dazzling lightly, nodding rapidly

25 Such a time of widening pace,
     Unlocking steps, peeping drowsily,
     Luring to see if damage was done
     Skipping down, trotting with banging
     Heart, checking frantically to note …

30 A bump of throbbing pain flew past
     Streaking across the shuddering body
     "What's all this?"

       The glory has departed
       Such the time it will stop;

35   When labouring days are gone
       Something is achieved, but Alas
       Now a part of masterpiece disappeared?
       Can't see why it is so,
       When time and hope wane,

40   Deep-rooted foot dangling foolishly,
       As all was abandoned, forgotten
       For nature's cause is greater than mortals'
       Fruitless search, leading to nothing,
       Nothing, until then resignation takes over

45   Agony of days recedes by,
       Each one adding to a poor soul's grief
       Like broken pieces of china
       Toy to a curious kid,
       What is to be done?

50   Accumulated sorrow in a bleeding heart,
       Flipping away from the dramatic scene,
        Tossing the remains of work from sight,
       Everything is halted, until comes again,
       Surely it will , power above shall help,

55   It will be restored, power beneath will help.
       Then, that time when running water
       Splashes, sobs of its rain drops, weeping,
       A careful peeping stops a moment's beat,
       Again, I dived to know what is to be done,

60   My hand touched a limp crumpled piece,
       Squeezed by angry arms,
       Yet, as it was not damned before,
       I sprang aloft and sat, trembling,
       Slowly, gently but firmly

65   Set aside the piece,
       Camouflaged in the cloak of drawing

Pieces, the work of weeks lay
Hidden. At last, the marauding
Masquerades have been blown up,

70 The time is reset for great work
To start,
Such was the time I heaved a sigh of relief

Prologue

Dislocation I

Rusting Plume

1   We have travelled fast
    Past my lands, ridden on snowy blizzards,
    Crossed many fountains and thickets,
    Withstood cleavages of the underworld,

5   We have returned to our places
    Where the black sun shines
    Pregnant moon, source of disaster,
    What shall we do but dwell therein,
    They are our land, the

10 Golden sovereignity of our father's world,
    All the stars have turned to blood,
    When we came back,
    Looked at the rusting season
    Wild plume of faded flowers,

15 A vengeance from the higher ones,
    Settling among us, tormenting,
    We are not to flee,
    We were born here, long
    Years ago, dazzling streak brilliantly shining

20 That was then, not now, things have altered,
    We are to face what we see
    The rust shall continue, the tide running fast,
    We are not to heave,

25 Our glory has gone but we shall dwell in our land
    We will dwell where we were born

Prologue continued

Dancing to the Rhythm

II

1 That was time buried by age,
  The vision of it coming to sight,
  Of the past lost, forgotten,
  Upon the high godly crest,

5 Where the immortals dwell,
  It gave way to a devastation,
  Thro' it, all were thus engaged,
  For who will be the ruler,
  Of who shall be the monarch,

10 When it ravaged, a fire caught alight,
   Fragments of burning nectar from the
   Past, recently sipped,
   Oh, grand Ichor is falling, spilling
   Down from heavenly palaces,

15 Like rolling dew of misty water,
   Trotting at heel, savaged trunk of 'Olupe'
   Wild ambition to rear higher,
   That was the case when we heard
   Dawn shaded by mystic drums

20 Looking like skinned hunters, lurking,
   Crowding all the sinewy lands
   What shall we do but dance to the tune?
   What is life if not to join the band?
   We are to do nothing but "dig the show"

25 Where we were bred had made it true,
   Our hands matted with blood of war,
   That was the time we began to see,
   Nothing was left but to join the crowd

All the plumages had burned, the
30 Land is shaking, quaking terribly,
    What are you to do but follow the
    Hand that brought it

Vengeance in Disca-World

III

1 The broad heavenly horizon down the west,
   Joining the wretched of earth-born,
   Kagara ranges, they raced past,
   Through deep alley crossing –

5 Bewildered landmark
   The dancing stead of savage power
   Can they check the wastage?
   Fountains long ago, where Titans abode,
   Where the milky glory was formed

10 Vanished when we soiled our
   Childbirth, the birth right of our fatherland
   Crystal azure of golden sky
   Can't hide them

15 Thus we have wandered,
   Into forests of fate,
   Casco wooded logs of bumping earth,
   All have gone wrong,
   Immortal path of human image,

20 When they dwell and know where
   They are, undimmed nature has
   Gone cursing,
   Laughing
   Splicing our unworthy life;

30 When even they themselves know,
   Meadow and slogged track of
   Our blissful contentment,
   Can they save the loners?
   We have o'er lapped the flipping

35 Wind, swift to carry us to the unknown,
   The sun has set,

The moon cascading wildly,
Phantoms of vengeance among us,
Grotesque shapes of our wonderment,

40   We are sliding back
Stepping on broken gravity,
Our velocity crushing stumps
Of sharp hope
The bitter edge shall receive us,

45   Are we to go back
Where?
Our motherland has been soiled,
When the natives were studying the truth
We have clung for so long.

50   Can't we stand on two mortal feet?
The cliff is shallow, steep and scrappy,
Down, we plunged over the
Edge of starlit Hades

Plunging over the weary world,
Over the edge that leads to titan's abyss,
Eye of winter storm
Pallas of savage eyes,
Flashing breastplate of immortal flame,
Apollo of grazing horses
Of stars, moon and sun

Dislocation IV

Nemesis: Metaphysical Beings

1 ... Let the flock glamour in their chirping,
 ... When the sun blackens the surface,
 ... Look, the stars are vanishing thinly,
 ... Upon the golden dawn that raced,

5 ... Shadow of meadow beaming, beaming
 ... Unforgettable sultan of Kante
 Like when they looked down,
 Seeing the suppression of man,
 Inequality, our watchword,

10 Creeping like elms, trying vainly
 To survive the gallant waves of immortal sea,
 Deep into the watery grave,
 Upon the Roof of Demon's Grove,
 Like when they sent the spy

15 To know if we shall remedy the error,
 But lo! The time has gone,
 Gone, miraculously disappeared in
 The grey cloud, gathering like the
 Savage myth of earth borns,

20 Winter storms, that roll and
 Split like cracking air,
 Its anguish felt by a million throats
 Sprawling you to the abode of darkness?
 Engulfed by dewy rain drops

25 Of cheeky tears, Plunged
 Over the bridge of black malting,
 When we behave like drones
 Changing with nature, molding
 Naked tits in our scarlet lips,

30 Still unable to rinse and
    Bail the neck-deep water,

II

Our lands are like desert,
Swept away by harmattan blow
"Unfertilized by out cropping of wary

35 Transgressors, the ancient nemesis,
    Mother of fatality
    Sister of the raging furies,
    Snakes ringed daughter of Cronos
    Flowing blood

40 That infest upon the oppressor,
    Chastising with edges of scorpion
    ...The flies have come back!
    ...See, they have brought it again
    ...We told them to leave the herb
    ...We are tired of following weary steps
    ...That brought nay but suffering
    ...Now it is late to join the walkers,
    ...We have accepted the atrocious defeat,
    Surrendered at the tip of the spear of justice,

45 The glittering armour raised with dexterity,
    Gleaming dazzlingly over the sunny slope,
    Probing into all nooks and crannies,
    When the flapping feather caught
    A dirty magnesia that held it,

50 Flipping of the shadowy skeleton,
    Struggling for existence upon moody
    World, until they passed and saw
    The premature shit that clutches
    With retreating hand on unhealthy ground,

55 And twice descended it,
    Our mortal flow split over alley,

Blackening, worsening, intermingling
With twigs that held fast, waiting
For our panting soul torn by

60 Parlous struggle and palaver ravage,
We are beyond repair!
We must face the dogma of death

Unconsoled Bird

V

1 I was a shabby bird crying,
   When my poor mother vanished,
   Many tried to console me,
   But I fled away from mortals

5 Gasped and wailed aloud,
   Little water, little running brook,
   The shrieking, clanging and banging of the wood,
   Lying in delirious nightmare, the
   The root where I sat was

10 Uprooted, carried by bloody shadows
   Of darkness, my poor sight strained,
   Longed to see the sun rise brightly
   Again, and dazzle once more for me,
   In a helluva lot, lost in labyrinth,

20 My clamouring and fluttering can do naught,
   Ere sundown in another world,
   We flew over to see our shore,
   To call back the baleful thing,
   It mingled with the horizon,

25 Blacking the utopian wet world,
   We hurried back, before the black thunder
   Raises fast, bubbling waves,
   Full shadow has impregnated animosity,
   In bondage

30 I was crying again to be heard,
   Motherland is not well
   But have they returned from their journey?
   What have they brought but abuse
   Plumage of uniformity led astray,

35 The unquenchable dawn of the immortal ones,
    Registering shadows of phantom in
    Our image, I continued to bark, wail,
    Groan and moan, a strong devil wind
    Bore the weak feather down with

40 Throbbing crash where we lay panting
    Coiled up, gyrating wildly, lost in the insane
    Blast of ecstatic pain
    My throat is bursting: have I achieved
    The set goal?

Where are the Illegally bought Fighters?

1   There he stood,
    Like the undaunted monument of Achilles,
    Sparkling with heavenly vigour
    Snarling at the shadowy crest

5   Where he was born, brandishing a hatchet
    Calling on all the magic of sorcery
    Bounding the bulging breast
    Incantating like an ominous beast
    Alas, has he grown no, or yes,

10 One naked pot was raised,
    To show the part to play,
    Oh farthest water of boulder's shore
    Running slowly, irritated by my presence,
    The gate of Hades was ajar,

15 From where the bloody underworld begins,
    Wounded mortal hearts ebbing their flow,
    Scalping sword, glittering like unburnished gold,
    Thrusting in willful vengeance at vacuous space,
    "Advance, stand back, lest we be pursued"

20 The dull phantom made a jerk
    A spasm-like jerk to polish an acacia trunk
    Alas, they were begging, banging,
    Clanging with metallic ardour,

25 The gods have fled at their sight,
    Jumping into thickets and vengeful cleavages
    The alley of mystery world or Lotos –
    There, blanketed by the skull of death
    'Twas hence from knee to breast,

30 Moonlit sprays danced where the trunks lay
    Breathing of wicked nectar, groaning,
    Writhing with hellish bliss

II

The serpent struggled, was unshackled
When the peeping dawn arose,

35 Unyoked at the gasp of 'nderi'
Scouring, skirting where to land,
The sun has risen; arrowing down vigorously
Blinking at the devils, to await the wretched ones
On the mountain top towards the abode,

40 Upon the ranges of flea-smitten hills
Where the dwarfs came to claim rulership
Alas, sat a jiggered rag of ambition,
A smiling, gleaming, burning tornado

45 'Crescendoing' blast upon all and sundry
Pouring down with vengeance from the sky borns
Burning with quaking hands to cling
To you, the undaunted figure at the hill
The world heard it coming

50 Amadioha is thunder bolting, the
Winter – storms of the earth – borns
Ravaging the enchantable 'Alomas'
The chink – chink – brow beater,
Unaffected by the bolter's weapon,

55 When the last blow descended

III

Niche and crash, bound to bound,
Crack and fiend, loud and loud,
Surfing the angry blizzards of yester years,
Spraying on running feet, thundering to hell,

60 Bramble of fog, leap of frog,
Skeleton of baboon, mound of harvest,
All, all shall bow to the quavering toe
Righting evil – cry of the wronged side,

Where are the black Hades – bound ones?

65 Songsters that promise to advance,
The serpent – infested head of Gorgon,
Thousand eyes, shakes of the Cyclops
That came to help and lost their identity,
Where is Amadioha's clap?

70 Or Ojukwu's leprosy arrow?
On one rugged soil, with metaphysical
Daring, where are they?
People we pursued from older-world
To roam and sprinkle the ashes on them,

75 For the iniquity to be abolished
What about those already dead,
Alone, raged the unfallen comrades
To visit justice on the sons of creeps

80 Alone to bear the fate of immortality?

Woman Nature - Cursable

1   I am the mountain
    Standing like a giant–walker,
    In the midst of crowding undergrowth,
    Exercising my power over mysteries of the dim past

5   Blazing like a horrified bull on seeing a predator,
    Crushing the abodes with wonderment,
    I am the river, swallowing rising eels,
    Flooding over the fields of mortals,
    Razing their subsistence to newer depths

10 In the watery grave where I lay
    Assailed but not wounded,
    Among the jagged rocks that tremble,
    Crack and wallow, a moving wave
    Of tempest,

15 I am the thicket, covering the world,
    Hiding the vegetation- ample one,
    Refusing owls that ominously hoot,
    Ere the downfall of wicked men,
    Altering nature with my eerie cries

20 Deep into bough-infested horizon, that
    Blaze like intense stars
    I am the sun, the sky born
    Appearing in winter month, accompanied by
    'Alles', son of Apollo,

25 Smiling upon the lower people,
    Ruminating intelligently with mystic force,
    Many cried for my woeful doing,
    Cursing the glowing diamond,
    Among a thousand dragons –

30 Alas, my dazzling defies
    The running water of dew tears,
    When I mingled with the razing

Dam,
I am the naked moon,

35 Pregnant, exposed to the immortals'
Wrath, being fragile, succulent
And vulnerable among our Azure cloud,
My hope lies in the 'Ilo' where
Children play and mothers curse,

40 The birth givers, all are earth
That supplies the heaving sigh,
This hereditary outlook of legendary world!
My mysteries are doubtful,
My will like racing flight,

45 I circle, engulf and plunge,
Headlong into watery den, dwindling ...
When stashes of boughs have gone,
And the moon perished at the
Self silent mask of clouds,

50 In the hands of shambling mothers?

The Vengeful One,
I Once Knew Him

1   When I was fluttering in the void,
     Dancing to the rhythm of the hallowed sound,
     The monologue of mystic drums,
     Quaking and racing in the tangy night,

5   Oblivion in slumber-sleep,
     We have scorched the better part of him,
     Carried the force that writhes endlessly,
     The hips gyrating wildly in ecstatic pain,
     Oh the scarlet venture,

10   The face of masking devil,
     The ample-dive of a long throated killer
     Race, decorate the banging chest,
     Over the bar, crossing innumerable rivers,
     The sacred nectar plunderer

15   The dread of mammalians
     That long ago we were told,
     Was I not IN the midst of them when it
     Chanced, ere 't came back
     Upon human vampire, feeding on

20   Swelling blood, split like flooding rain,
     On the madness of false image,
     The ROOT was born again,
     Obstinate, intractable, the voice of one
     Walking in the dark field of

25   Roundabout world, crying hysterically,
     A series of womanly bunch,
     But lo! What was its birth like?
     When the royal iguana's blood was
     Sweet squeezed from a sprawling slave,

30 Dazed submissively to the will of the master
    It appeared; sprayed, carrying a body,
    Covered in mysterious shroud, the shroud
    That grows to nemesis – the transgressors,
    Chasing after rainbow in the far west,

35 All, all took to evil flight,
    Flying to where and when I
    First knew him.

Lyrics and Other Traditional Longer Poems

The **Archaic**, faded, thatched hut
Designed with human skull,
Invisible to the human eyes,
Unreflecting in the sunlight,
Is the residence of the sorcerer

The staggering, bent, old magician
Wrinkled in the morning sun,
Fearless in the darkness,
Sluggish in movement
Performed many types of rituals

Dangering the villagers with
His powerful, evil spiritual
And satanic powers
The magician is on his journey

Alone in the dark night,
Walking in the small, grassy path
The sorcerer mumbled meaningless words
To human ear but meaningful to him

The owls and falcons striking
Their dangerous hootings are
Used as an instrument
To warn the villagers about
The appearance of this ageless monster,

With the dazzling morning sun,
Striking fear to the entire villages
With his usual terrible cry
The old sorcerer awakens the dawn
With powerful move he renders
Thunderbolt no the face of the clan
To announce the opening of the new day

2   In the dark, dim, grey light of the 'Aladum',
Reflecting two dark shadows on the wall
One male, one female,
So as to keep away

The searching and repulsive eyes
Of the snoopers,
The two teenage lovers
Engage in their lovemaking

To knock on the door
While this is going on
Is the proverbial wasting of precious time
Understanding about the mood in which
They were, the riddle beyond many

The high powered light of the 'Aladum'
Portrays that the work is done,
So male or female can ask or enter
The going verse about the riddle
In itself a lifelong job

"Who's that?" is the question
That follows the present knocking
"Enter, if you like"
Then know that their want
Has been satisfied

3   It seems as if it is in
A dream, a sleep or a nightmare
No, it is the last
In the sleep of the troubled man,
Appearing to him is the god of death,

Then, why is he appearing?
To take him or what
What the man is seeing is
A force of superstition
Coupled with supernatural beliefs

How can it be possible?
An open coffin with a dead human being
Horror at his side
What, what has he done?
He sees blood and fire everywhere,
Is it the end of him?

Dangerous mammalians, age-long animals
Hanging in the window place
In the smokey fire, dancing naked
Seem to be the female ones
With their breasts held in their hands

He sprang up from his bed
What is happening to me? he queried
Then, in a moment he seems
To be lost in a delirious mist,
Everything seemed lifeless,
Stars, he saw, revealing ominous danger
Evil spirits, he saw them, black,
With their bodies covered with thorns,
Eyes as big as eggs
Am I to die?

In the dreadful silence of the night
He heard the wicked owl hoot
Oh! He cried, it is the end of me
But now too and, alas,
He heard the drumming of the dead,
Of course, it is the chief, his uncle,
Has died
So the chief did him
All this before dying

He fell down,
Foaming in the mouth
Gasping for breath
He murmured, "help, power from above and beyond", To
his surprise the day broke
He saw the rays of the sun
From the cracks through
The roofings of the house
He thought of the last night's experience
He fainted ...

4   In the old, warlike age of Africa
    When the heavenly built African people

Eased their life with hunting
And spiritual havocs,
The fertile soil of Africa
Grew the most beautiful crops in the world,

The warlike people of our fatherland
Fought back the growing influence of the white race,

The period of colonisation in Africa
Coupled with slavery,
The transfer of African beautiful blood
To new lands,

Your cries were heard all over the world,
The inhumanization you suffered
Under your heavy burden
The scars all over your body,
The whip they used to chastise you,
The hot tropical sun you work every hour,
The suffering of Africa is never a good tale

The strong ropes that bound you
Will be broken
The whip and weapon that were
Used to treat you mercilessly
Will be broken,
The oppressors that led you out under the sun
Like sheep of sacrifice will be quenched
The mourners of African suffering will be consoled

The oppressors will be trodden upon,
The narrow path broken by them
Will be narrowed
The path of incredibilty
That blindfolded the eyes
Of people will be removed

The African continent is growing well
Among many ancient civilisztions,
The way to independence is being achieved

5   In the deep, hollow water of the clan
Over the cliff that covered the path
Lived the mammy water

The mysterious, devilish and superhuman witch
Was responsible for every loss of life
And havoc in the sorrounding areas
Dried lizards, eggs, manillas, chameleons and tortoises Were
used as objects to appease the wrath
Of the sorcerer,
Yet repercussion prevails

In the bottom of the sea,
Covered with all sorts of human parts,
Decorated with evil-smelling Elaginas
Is Alopate with the incredible eye
That kills the naked eyes that see it

The legendary 'Onye ga si' creeping out
In the village, unknown,
Headed for the sea,
Wriggling in the moonlight shadow

The brave man entered the sea,
In a swift movement
Coupled with anxiety
To see the witch, the fearless man shouted
Over the head, a dangerous bird
And the witch passed,

And perching on a nearby grass
Screamed
The man dived at the wretched creature
But in time to see
A huge grave dug in his front

"The queen ruler of the sea,
Possessor of mysterious powers
Pray, I beseech thee to pardon thy impetous one
If thou should sin not,
For thy heavy power

If thou loosed thy wrath upon
The pieces of the golden clay
Could it not be felt?

The animosity in the witch's heart
When she is half-human,
Half-animal
Heard the Libation
Thy sons poured to thee

Move the soul of the intelligent world,
Thee that thy creepers sent
To fortell the power of thy queen glory!
If I were to leave you
The story of thy bravery be revealed
To all human race!

In a swift dash she held 'Onye ga isi' down
Into the deep water
They went in and were seen
No more for ages
Till the time of the Nri Dwarfs

Song of the Nri Dwarfs

6   The great power of the ruling class,
The neglect that was loosed upon us,
The outcast dwarfs still cry
To the human race,
The smaller in stature
Will they live?

Their sorrow came to me,
Oh! King of Nri,
The powerful dwarf that destroys and saves,
The great maker of justice
Why, thou, let your race
Be treated like that?
The taller humans treated
Us as though with dishonour
Why are we not buried

According to tradition?

Sweeping, toiling all night
We toil
Yes, we did it,
But see the humans destroy us
Oh! How to show ourselves to thyself?

The King's Reply

"Wait, have patience,
Peace and restoration is at hand
The mammalian society that treated thou so,
Will be crushed

The rejection attributed to your dwarfness
Will be destroyed
The untouchables will be consoled
For my power will be felt evenly on
Breathing ground and land

Dry your eyes, you shall,
Yes, you shall rule
The face of the earth

From the high mountain place
My dwelling palace,
I heard your cry of sorrow,
I, the god of thunderbolt, although small,
And dwarfish, will show the whole race
That power is power
Witch is witch, magician is magician,
Supernatural is all the same
But small or no small
Thy power will be felt

I, your mighty King
Do not want to see sorrow on your face
The time to retaliate and react is at hand
Yes, it is at hand"

He called all his powers
Thunder! Thunderbolt!
Went down
To evacuate the face of the earth

The earth trembled
Mountains, trees, houses, and forests
All quaked and shook the whole race
Of humans
Who turned to tumulting and stampeding
As they felt the power of the head dwarf

Down, under the earth
The king of the dead dwarfs
Let out fire with his mouth
Which swept past the race that
Causeth the greatest abomination
To his people

7   Perilous, it now came, please,
Life moving as a dream,
Marvelous is essential
For man lives in the
World of trouble free mind
Alas, but come see an Ogbanje
That has a restive spirit

"Mother", he muttered
"They have come again"
Now, what his eyes met, indescribable,
Women of age, advanced, naked

Yes, he saw them, in his sleep, naked,
Sitting on stools, with half-gourd in their hands,
Blood! Yes, he saw blood inside the gourds
Oh! They are presenting it to him
What is he to do?

"Oh, mama, please get a knife and gun
They killed me", he shouted and woke
Now, came the tragic scene

In his imagination
He saw water and white people,
Hair long, naked, swimming,

He is to come there
Impossible
Now, dancing in the heavy, moving blood
Are the boys
Are they human beings?
Possibly not
How can they be?
They seem to be dragging him up

To lands of devils, he went
Horror!
Shame upon bad spirits
Here they came again,
Knives up, holding them to strike
He fell to the ground

The boy said:
"Now came the heart and ten heads"
He cried
His body mingled with blood,
Shouting in front of him,
Alas, the powerful magicians
Creeping towards the poor boy
Ordering him,
Spitting on every site
And muttering all evil words
He advanced

Kernel oil and 'Ogirish' leaf
Were being applied on the boy,
Then, what next?
Bouncing downward,
Raising the superhuman chap,
Flung it, and out it went forever

8   In the broad heavenly, huge peak,

Thundering day and night,
With his coarse voice
The king of the gods dwells,

Land of strange beings,
Though human in a way
That is, sleeping and eating,
Immortal souls with their deathless spirit

Yes, the lame ones most dangerous of them,
Answer the iron breaker
And roaring voice like flame of fire
Of their great and mysterious father and leader

Pouring evil witchings on the wrong verse,
Using the ancient thunderbolt
Of their fore great Pregas,
The great high mountain god
Satisfies himself

The beautiful daughters of the heavenly place
Once appeared in their precious garments
With their wings behind them
Their uncovered, maturing breasts reveal
That their prime age is being approached

Superstitious and supernatural beliefs
Reveal that attempting,
Not succeeding,
To engage
In any art of love on the immortal souls,
The pursuing spirit of powerful Sugas
Retaliate in the blackness of the day

Yet immortal, the waist of the
Daughters are uncovered,
But for the beads and other heavenly products
The mixture of herbs and powerful ointment
Of white and black trace shows indigo signs

The charming sisters put suffering to all their lovers
If any of their mysterious blood is seduced
Land is there to placate the rest of the troublers
With the hooting of the Asies
The evil bird marking
Their approaching and coming

The early farmers hid behind the trees
To watch the beautiful sisters
Gathering their rose flower
With searching eyes,
Then compensation was the case

9   That's it, the fearful season,
Yes, it is the heart of the rainy season
With episodical and tragic happening
The moon gone, the sun shone thinly
The stars all disappeared in the gloomy cloud

The most perilous and horrible time of it
No moon in the hollow sky
The darkness fell before its time
The long process of night was dangerous

No play in the Ilo,
No singing, no dance in the arena
No activity functioning in the clan
Fathers gave stern warning to their children

That's the time, evil spirits roaming
The entire surface with searching
Eyes and deadly sneer
Even the greatest and mysterious
Witch doctor and medicine man
Went to bed early

For no earthly creature
Could withstand the glory
Of the deathless beings
Immortal, invincible,
Superstitious, unreal, incredible

10 Barbaric and vandalistic motions
Were not yet prevailing
The monstrous shedding of costly
Human blood is in practice,

Power to shift was decided by war
Hissing in derision and eyeing in askance
Was a common ritual
Communal killing of innocent creatures
That they called 'Ogbanje'
And twins was not interrupted

The most incredible that should be banished,
Was the slaughtering of innocent people –
Yes, they were killed like goats
When the traditional chief
Vacated the human realm
To the spiritual and deathless world

The tragic happening that accompanied
This episodic mystery was still
A question that must be solved

No silly movements,
No normal business functioning,
Tappers, the poor creatures that suffered most,
Their gourds fixed to the palm trees were forgotten
Even if overflowing to last forever there

The high powered charm
And medicine of those that lived
To check the unexpected movement
Of powerless, useless and hopeless villagers

Who did nothing but submit
To whirling power,
That drove lives and caused
Change to the harmattan season

To treat them with maturity,
Tyrannical, despotic and lunatic land evolved

Even the poor old men
Were pursued into the forest

For the women, gangs of armed men
Led them to the stream for water usage
Nyaya, the unaware stranger
Mumbled to himself
After drinking,
While making his way towards the village

Knew nothing of the chief's recent death
His walking stick, he beat the bush with
Powerful words pouring out
Meaningless vows to unseen spirits

Like lunatics, powered by the spirit of ecstasy
And powerful herbal mixtures
The warriors pounced upon him
While rope was snagged upon his neck
He was slashed to the 'abo'
And soon was carried
To be put where lay the dead chief

With hideous cruelty
He was slaughtered like a sheep
For sacrifice
His dumped body was pierced
With sharp, thirsty blades

While he said goodbye to all mortals,
The repulsive creatures went unchallenged
With questionable motives

11 In the stillness of the blackest night
That portrayed some mysterious happenings
The people of the valley listened attentively

Over them hung the huge range
Of mountainous peaks
Inhabited by wild
Ageless and deathless apemen

With great physical and luminous
Ways of life

In the valley, created by the range
Lay the disappearing race of double skinned
Huge human beings
Yet their fear of the mountainous beasts
Created perplexity
In the small thatched hut
Nothing visible could be seen
For darkness covered everywhere
Only for the tiny, fading light
That kept the wild beasts away

Nyang! Imuyoug! Pasanigo! Onnah!
Roared the hoarse voices
Of the apemen
That echoed through
The Imuanyu congregation
The archaic language was meaningless
To human ear
Yet the chemical portion of it
Was full of unexplainable sayings

The terrible voices roared again
The Okoko hooted now
The shrill voice of creeping beasts
Was also noticed,
Cold fever seized everybody
The powers of deathless
Super beings were intolerable

12   Here, they come
He could see a small congregation
Of fierce professional warriors
All dressed in a strange way
'Omu' all over their body
With 'Uyi' painted, scattered patterns
Looking beautiful,

Dazzling knives spurted in the air
But what happened in front
Seemed poor compared
To the twisting of armoured ritual

On their heads they carried the coffin
The dead corpse,
With the shrouded clothes
Accounted for the ominous sign

They moved not with human power
The dead 'Ikpa' man directed them
Yes, he was killed yesternight

It was a witch that
Caused the unbelievable act
That struck the warrior
The power that suppressed the best
Unreality that showed evil sign

Could it be believed?
It took place,
Four men held now

With surging force
It trusted with remarkable force
The shackle was intolerable
The power, superhuman
The carried body vibrated
It quaked

The earth trembled
The cock crowed
Breathing of the world stopped
While all stopped dead

The corpse rose again
During their wary, ritual dance
The new game in the arena
He cried aloud
And let go of the corpse

He fell face downwards
Foaming in the mouth
Yes, 'Ndakwu-kwu'
A terrible disease

The continuation was inevitable,
The sporting was normal
Collapsing was violent and frequent
But nothing like this had ever happened

13 The evil forest that rules all
The entity beyond human understanding
We, of simple life, shudder
The remover of life when sweetness comes
Powerful judge that blasted the wild
Indelible rhythm that quaked the world
The possessor of mysterious twitching

The founder of occult world
The power that shines visibly
He floods with wide steeps
But, loo, is thy forgiveness this?

Thy mind trembles,
The shrill cries of the oppressed
The restorer with inhuman power
Invisible oracle that strikes

They came in groups
The Great Spirit that caused omen
Drought inheritor, leprosy issuer
The swollen belly carrier,
The throbbing pain distributor

Thy power that hooked the clan,
The way to solve overgrowing mysteries
The unheard of has taken place
The fishy fluid that produces human life
The dry patch that fuels the "black death"
What doneth we?

Mournful harvest,
Suicide impositor
The creeper that held the breath

The sun showered dully
The moon gone
The sky gloomy
Eye, the roamer of evil world,
That was sent by you,

The troubler of the human race
By thy springy step
You kill in a twinkle

They give not you thy share
The greedy men of Qumja Bay
The great fathers
Have mercy on your beneficiaries,
Lessen your mighty hand on us

14   The rose flower of the high crest
That shines upon the mortal world
The giver of fruitful sensation
The dazzling clothes of young teenagers
The embroidered velvet of superhumans
The twinkling sun you sent early enough
The heat of the sand seemed unbeatable
They have treated them unfairly
The long drought had almost devoured all eatables

The way to death is open for you
Going forward, the thorn bush lies,
Backwards, the monster devours
The way out is not thinking of crowing
Among one another

The hurling of the javelin
The tormentors notice not what comes,
Up, it went, and disappeared
In the bright sunlight

The high place it went,
Then the sharp point of the sharp blade
Pierced the fragment of the daughter
And outflows the mortal blood ('ichor')
The alley she went
And with deep cracking she rose up

Up she swept again and came
With indignation from her heavenly father,
"Thou wicked creatures that treated me so
The blood of one daughter shall be avenged"

The oily "Bikana" of herbal products
The creepers brought and rubbed
On the fatal wound,
it healed

The grand fate and furies were sent
To decapitate the ambitious sons of mine
Their wing opened
The cloak of their labour flew
The flippers came down
They fled to the congregation
of wrecked creatures

The turning verse was immeasurable,
The pitiful note came upon them,
The rain and tornado they saw
The sun continued,
The drought raged on,
But the anger was not appeased

The pestilence marched on the beasts,
The locusts destroyed greenish leaves
The anger was not appeased

He glared with his approach
The left burdener turned back
The owners were chased against
The rushing rivers on the steep bank

Going back, mutual death,
Going forward, painful death,
The elms were uprooted,
The rushing stream raged like a bull,
The god of river that devoured quick,

The dangerous Sirens and Errinyes,
Were still there while the men
Crowded the steep slope,

The lightning flashes,
The thunderbolt of heavenly father booms,
Wind rose from the earth,

Victims of death cried horribly
Horned beings with black traces emerged,
With decorated spears and knives in hands
While they looked for their preys

The horror-striken people ran down the edge
Keeping watch like ants,
The ruler rose again
And fate seized them
The water flung itself on them
While the horned men opened mortal skulls

The few left flew on water,
The children cried,
The men mourned,
The world stopped still

This was about 20000 years ago,
The great vengeance that troubled the natives,
The great leaf that quaked the ground,
The wonderful torpedo that followed undisturbed,
The wave of nature that swept past them

15   The splitting continues,
      The heaps turned up and trembled
      The quaked grounds,
      The smell of blood scented air

While vultures covered over
The gloomy and cloudy sky,
The beautiful flowers of the nation
Vanished instantly
The young, promising teenagers
Crept like the trembling doe

The work of the day showed
Humiliating attitude
Turning round and round
The escapees
Covered in dewy mist

Forward surged the wicked murderer,
Backwards, the god of river was against him,
The turning Jems reached the peak,
He stood, shaking like a trampled beast
His weight leaving him

The perilous dilemma seemed unending
If he went forward
Brutal and non-mortal death,
If he went backwards
Prey to the demons that devour quick
Who will surely scavenge on him

The sharp corner that hid him,
Then, like a powerful breeze
He turned to see the dazzling machetes
Flying above the tormentors' heads,
He stood still with horror
While the blackness of the day
Turned against him,

With powerful, violent force
They brought it down on his head
Exposing his brains
He sank, clutching at the bloody wound,
They brought it down again and again
While his strength escaped him

He stretched on his hopeless attire, helpless,
They rose up, the secret ones and tremblers
The vengeance was unpardonable,
The quick action of immortal rulers was revealed

The verdict of them was given thus:
"May the sun shine upon that day,
Yes, the day that heralded it,
A male child was conceived,
May the sky be gloomy and cloudy,
The day be cursed and be unaccounted for
May it seek sunshine and see none,
The stars be dim and
Perpetual darkness operate
The hooting of the wicked owls
Be heard and awaken the dawn

"When the marauding savages were born,
The worthless evil pursuing good
Be the order of the day,
May they have no rest
Until costly mortal blood is avenged,
The fugitiveness and the vagabondness
Of the sentimental Ocios
Be better than this,
The time of the arrival be not announced,
Then, they turned sharply in the moonless night,
May they vanish into thin air
And may not the great ocean of Poseidon
Cleanse their blood spurted,
Brutal, garish hands
And may they die prematurely"

16 'We meet to part, and part to meet
Till we meet to part no more'
The son of men that possess tribal affiliation
On them,
Yet, the seeming rose-like smell of rose flower,
Nothing that was undone,

You sons of wicked men

When we took them,
Urian and Thumin, do fall upon them
But when they guessed how they died
The thawing point was taken
The great queen of heaven
With Thesiman power rushed me
From the bank,

But yet, the wave of indelibility
Was greater than the
Force acting upon me

Her bank was covered with thorny bush,
The other way, full of raft
Iced by the marauders
The middle of it, among all the dead,
Silence prevailed

The cries of my children have reached me,
They will soon be led like shepherdless sheep
To the slaughter,
Their cry rent the air
Their mourning patrolled the sky less cloud,
What are we living for?
To seat idly while the heaps of their corpses
Made a mound, like yams
Why not die saving my family flocks?

Sharply and swiftly he turned
And brandishing the spherical matlock,
He whirled like the sweeping wind

The tied ones resumed their cries
As machete vs machete, matlock vs matlock
Rent the stillness of the air
And shattered the deathly silence

The interwoven force dwindled
They pushed forth to the valley

And it was the great stalemate,
No hope, nervousness
Overshadowed the muscular bodies
Overconfidence killed the knowledge of man

Brutally, he fought for the salvation of his family
The first blow exposed a man's skull
Guttered, the debris and human blood
Rushed like water,
Made up of living organisms

Falling to the ground
Last animalistic, inhuman and metallic gasp
Escaped his throat
As they second closed his eyes in darkness,
Rushing waves swept him off
And distantly he flew

Horror-stricken, looking like Omen
He wanted to kill, to kill the wanted
But still he fought on,
The third blow of the matlock
Savaged the windpipe, sawing it off
The neck was chopped off
While the gullet
Was like raging anarchy

Children, wives, relatives,
All flew like the wind
To avoid the wrath of the senders

17   The springing water rose up,
The elms doing their mysterious darting
In their beautiful pool
Felt the scorching heat

The bank grew cold
Yet perpetual fire scorched the scales of the fish
The dark blue eyes of the leader
Changed to deadly, reddish colour,
The ruler of the ocean released

The tremendous impact
Issuing and blowing upon them,
The palace turned white,
Beautiful furniture turning brownish

The two guides opened their mouth
And let bombs of cold saliva
Down the hot atmosphere,
The situation seemed to be thwarted
For some minutes
But resumed – very forceful,
After gathering full force,
That lived beyond it

The air ceased
All seemed lifeless
As the hotness was felt
The brightly coloured herbs and sea-weeds
Changed their appearance
As the glorious queen appeared
They bowed in reverence
The tormentors that possessed
The inherited underworld,
Fled as the power appeared,
Now, she stood in gravely form
Heaving a brutal sign and spitting willfully
She cursed thus:

"You wreckage of nature,
The killer of tender hearts,
You who can think freely
But rejoice and delight
In the ending of human existence

"May you all be cursed,
The fruit of your labour be for nothing sake,
The sunshine of tomorrow
Will surely elude you,
Son's darkness,
Tormenting and humiliating experience

Be upon you,

"You destroyers of beautiful, dazzling lives
May the house of you
And the house of your fathers
Be brought to an abrupt
And unceremonious end
The ones left will be leprosy-infested
It is done, it is done".

18 It came rushing back
Like the harmattan sweeping wind,
The tale of the old,
So long that they recalled incredible things
In their high place

The handed down tradition
Quoted that the Iri people
Were congregating together
To form an ethnic group
Culturally and physically
Reigning there,

The high powered Irineshi stood,
The god of this rulership
Towered high above the crest of the nearest tree
At the foot, pieces of foodstuff offerings lay
The governing directors were loyal

Menace soon lay before them
A high, double skinned giant
With magical powers,
Armed and brandishing a hot machete
Rose it up and down

It fell an the nearest Iri
A cry of horror and shout
Of metallic amazement rent the air
As the beautiful, black blood
Flew on the grassy path
Lo! it descended again

While yet another fell;
The massacring continued,
Until the king appeared

He was encountered too
And alas, the bloody knife
Fell on the royal velvet
And tore the skirt of the robe
Much astonished, rather than dazed
Or stunned, the horror-stricken king
Crumbled on his knees
While, with the remaining motion,
The blackness of the day swept over him

He lay stretched there
Helpless and hopeless
The blood dripped,
The wound pained,
The body ached
While the hole in his head throbbed

The unheard had occurred,
The murderous giant, mad with killing
Rushed like the rising wind
And stood face to face with the Irineshi god

In his attempt to push it down,
There was a loud clap
The door of the heavenly sky opened,
Bombs of thunderbolts flew
And was followed by blinding, dazzling light

It fell upon the giant and sparked fire
On the huge monster
He started to burn
And was turned into mere ash

19 The nymph of the great heaven,
The orbs that crowded them,
The unstoppable, ominous vengeance
That creeps like a wild stag

The embroidered and furnished palace
Stood gentle and free
From others
Seemed nude when the morning rains struck

The heavenly palace
That secures the heavenly bodies
The echoes of the carthorse
And racing events thundered
In the mortal, shadowy world
Down, down, it moves
Until it touches the
Bottom of the earth
The shoal and shadowy
Hades that kept the deathless ones

It whirled like the contrasting wind
And moves gropingly
Again, it stumbles on the great pot
And poured the content out,

The nymphs dived for the dreamless world
But utter sleep reigns on the blackened place
They dived again
And the voice of the heavenly
Fathers called them forth

The rhythm now is fierce
And the metallic atmosphere here is dazzled
And stunned by the great celebrator
They sought for the death world
But the father called them forth,
Angrily and reluctantly, they came back
To the palace of the great ruler-god

The great alley dwellers
And the beautiful Thessians of the mountain side
The celebration was heated
As they entered with dull faces
And stood speechless and motionless

Surly expression on their ruined faces

They seemed ashamed
As they did not achieve their objectives
But stood like a forgotten god
Worshipped by an abandoned priest

They seemed not contented,
But alas and alas!
They angrily came back
And shook the great men

The whole bloody high crest
Started to vibrate,
They shook its foundation
They quaked the inhabitants
And did the impossible,

The bravery and boldness vanished
Into thin air
And nothing but the sound of tornado
Was heard,

They fell on their faces
And worshipped the great god
For the foolishness of their hearts

20 Suddenly, the sky became cloudy
And wore a sullen, heavy face,
The sun dimmed as the small
Penetrating light vanished,

The whole clan fell upon one another
And an oracle was literally consulted,
The deep remark of the god's messenger
Was ominous
Utter sincere crept like gathering, winding force
As utter darkness penetrated
Into the nooks and crannies of the clan

It was an avenging darkness, immortal, invulnerable
It bathed the small, chipping light,
The god of vengeance was operating
The oracle holder sighed
And turned towards the western sea

It was gloomy
And the small hooting of the owl,
Was heard,

It was the time of danger and all
Was seized by deathly silence
And insurmountable deadliness

It seemed like a scraping sound
The shadow of the former light vanished
Like sulfur-hydroxide
Helpless men saw the atmosphere's nature
And recollected the ancient sacrifices

Alas, the daughter of the king
Shall be slain and devoured
By the leading medicine men
And the incomprehensible god will be soothed,

The out-carting of it was slow,
Laborious process
And the queen and king cried
Themselves out
And watched with wondering,
Incredible and incredulous eyes
As their daughter's soul sped back to Hades
Lamenting her youth and womanhood

At last, the old priest appeared
And, throwing over his velvety shroud,
Like ambrosial gold, thunders:

"Ye, all you silent listeners,
All ye congregation of the heavenly powers,
Thundering day and night on thee,

What have ye done to deserve utter darkness?

But as thee lay and thy
Great power was felt
Receive from the poor seekers
The holy and virginal daughter,
Of thy anointed
Forget their past sins
That moveth thy anger
Receiveth it oh holy one
And stop blasting us
With darkness and thunderbolt
We pray thee"

The dazzling machete, raised and flashed,
The blazing light flowed everywhere,
The dazzling, beautiful virgin stood still
As the powerful thrust
Savaged the innocent one

The blood split on the holy floor
As she sank on her knees
And covered her head,
By utter darkness

She cried out in painful blast,
The god of sun and light resumed his work
And soon dazzling light was shown everywhere
As the formality and normality began
But the life of mortal remained a probability

21 Nature seemed uncheatable
As the bygone days sped
The life of the old warrior-heroes
Swept like flying wind

As the darkness eluded them,
Their eyes became dim
And their lives short-lived,
Although completed
It was hopeless

As the nature of oldness and retribution
Rang clearly and cracked
Like palm kernel in their ear

The time had just passed
The old, better days
When men were men
And women won by the hand
Of the bold and brave

The new eggshell that cracked now
Was invaluable,
Moral incapacity was the key
To the present generation's backwardness

The old heroes sighed in unquenchable rage
As they remembered the old "egg shell"
Of their times
The period when men here bold
And strong
When the state of affairs was well moving

Not now!
No, it is supposed not to be so
The laughing and the metallic sound
Of the music rhythm
And the moving into period of ecstasy
Was bygone product

It disappeared in the shadowy mountain
And the snow washed high crest
The echoing sound and unclimbable mountain range
Like unfulfilled archaeological excavation,

Nothing held the new children
From polluting and violating the laws of mankind
How merciful the heavenly fathers were
The wretched mortals that seemed to forget their past
Yet the dubiousness of the great vengeance
Will be done right

22   Stop evil emotions and divert from
Devious ambition, aspiration and usurpation
The wickedness of the new generation
Had endured, but forecast had been made
And the whole collaborators will be bound
With the ancient serpent
For one thousand years
In flame and consuming fire

It sprang up obstinately and stubbornly
Without heeding a sigh sign
It stood gigantically, like an outcast brave man,
The whole atmosphere was filled
With pleasant smell of roses
And the beautiful scent of the immortal flower

That's where it stood years past
Whenever the advanced
Recollection seemed unbelievable
The four-headed, one-eyed and seven-nosed monster,
The pricking was indeed superb
But the outcome miserable

The adventurous young man killed it
But the leprosy of the shining head
Escaped him not

There fell the Ichor like rain
And the hard ground was wet,
Yet, it continued to pour down
And swallowed the piercing eyes

Horror-stricken and half-dead,
He rose as the chattering forest roared,
The river answered,
The mountain cried out
As the insects of the forest chirped heavily
Showing million-million signs,
The path lay open
But running, the limbs no longer could carry

On the hollow pathway,
The black, dark god grew light
As the inhuman shape hid the trembling rays

The question was then revealed and many asked:
"Why did he do that"?
Broken and much disappointed
The brave retired to the deep sea valley
And hotly pursued by leprosy vengeance,
Vanished forever

Then where did he go?
The entity was hoarded
As the founders searched for the lost hero
They dwindled back and forth,
Lost their path and paid their penalty

23   The shining waters of the pleasant valley,
It was full of dazzling pebbles
That intrigued human looks
Leapt upon the narrow path
As he saw them with delightful interest

Such was the mocking ground
Where arose like battle combaters
And threw high rate of momentous noise
And silenced the singing falcons

Appear if you like and see
The end of human existence
Yet, he resolved to carry out the perilous operation
And trembled as the saliva spurted
Out from his meek mouth
But it opened and with
Changed heart
Muttered "Tubakarinami"
Idoha, the call of the temple god,
He invoked and waited patiently
To receive the power
The cold water whirled and the reeds shook,

The splashing was terrible
It seemed like wrecking ship

The water was beaten like snake
And lo, divided two
Revealing staunch grounds,

It appeared from the ground beneath,
The earth corners where the hot magma dwelled,
It was insightful as it sailed to the top sea
And stood gigantically above the creaking waves
The height was hidden and laden with force
It stood, four heads, with huge dissolving eyes
Watching the prey,

Three snakes, four baboons and five Jackals
Readied and waited for their command,
Hissing tongue poured out lava smoke
And singing sirens were focused on,

"Why don't you call us from the deep dream
That decided human nature,
What gaveth thee the unbroken power
Of interference and intrusion"?

All roared and closed their eyes
As they saw the wrecked mortals

He began: "Thy powers have been recognized,
The Hybolimiys of great river dwellers
Implore thee, thy reverence,
That the devouring battle goes on
And rolls side ways but mercy
For the poor,
Thy high look turns to stone people,
Look that is powerful in the face of all creation,
You liveth forever and rule for ages,
Unsurpassable great healer, mercy"

He brought out the evil destroyer
And in the high happiness

Of the monstrous sea dwellers
He hurled, swung, he threw
Pierced, it struck
And vengeance was completed

Howling cries roared and moaning cries were heard,
Water splashed, cracked rocks and sand rumbled
And sea elms trembled
The horrid smell doomed the doe
And tales of sorrow were unchallenged

The fiery cry of the smokey ranges,
The march of the sea storm
And the belting of animalistic sound,
The natives were under human control,
The jagged rock flew up
Blindingly
And flashes of crackling rumbles were noted

Slowly, lifting up to the great
Shallow deep water
Where their fathers lived
He cried for vengeance
And was swallowed by the rushing water

What was created to destroy the giants?
Was it diverting or was it accomplishing?
All was good and hissing
And with heavy, deadly sign
It was all over

24 Knowledge of an adversary was superb
It controlled the man with monumental force,
Yet, if there was any danger
It rang like fluent 'Ogene'
And sounded boomingly like hollow 'Ikolo',

The time came and passed
And nothing could he see or do
He looked like a dirty, neglected,
Jagged and broken pot

But his power among the governmental force
Was still retained

The superpower was firmly held by the horse reins
And the horns of a majestic rhino
But yet, he was looked down
Upon and laughed and scorned
Yes, why not

He was diplomatic, covering his sins
And iniquitous transgressions and evil doings
Among the senders' force
It was brutal like fierce Achilles
When Patroculus died
And as possessed as
Diomedes with Athene's power

He feared no one and respected no born man
But Fate and the furies were near
And doomed opulence was sprinkled into his life,

The way to Hades was easy,
But what's all this
It seemed make-believe and half actual
But yet the hope was deserting him
He was looked upon as a vigilante
But feared as a monster,

Flashes came with force
And human blood and brain quaked
Mixture flew and sprinkled
On the hard stone floor

25 Still they stood as they drew away
The dappled clothes,
The dangling breasts
That fed many lay down
And almost touched the fallen belly
The fullness of lustful womanhood had vanished
To become a poor, forgotten old thing,
The brown nipples were no longer succulent

Indeed, a lot was encountered
And many sorrowful experiences seen,
The round waist was pious
But the swollen belly that
Created many individuals was old

Oh! What a terrible sight,
The former curved hip was out of its torso angle
And the thin, stricken legs were inhuman,
Oh merciful, why was her nature so changed?
But soon the issues came to rescue her
And save the great work of creation

26 Why was it so?
It was rippled and almost like the new age
It was almost unforgettable as it was noticed
By the new generation
It was an old tempered eggshell,
Yes, it was at the highest point
And incubator was needed if not nativity,

Was the old hen realizable and attentive?
Maybe not, for why was it so?
As it bore no such remark
And bore no reproach

It exploded in the long silence
And chicks stepped out from the cracked life
Eyes closed and ears thin
Power was "eludable" as the old producer
Came to attend to the producer

And consumers who were
Not brought up according to nature
As the mother was beheaded anyhow
Can't it be changed?
Like the reciprocal metallic sound
Of the piercing town crier's metal gong
Renting the air with its vibrating force

Who to blame?
"Motherland people
Or the waxing of high western education
And colonial civilization

The two sides that fought over our soul
The new egg that cracked was unblamable
And the sound unforgettable
Its power, incredible and almost piercing

27 Here it goes
When there was metallic laughter
In the atmosphere,
It drizzled and poured down
In hot, subtle torrents
Alas, it echoed through
The evil possessed state

The ravaging time was at hand
And hardly enough for immortal creation,
That's the time
It was piercing, but shadowy and moody
Like a fallen herd, roaming about
In the cracking ground
Face to face with one jagged figure
That bellowed tantalizingly:
"What's done was poisonous"

"Ma'am, what's what?"
The time was late
As the imaginative brain
Worked quickly

"Mercy for thy offending strength seemed good"
 "Look back and see Criporus
Why then do they trail so deep
In the land of Hades?"

"Look back and see Fairies and Fairies"
"What a sight"

Skeletal mammalians with
Heaving monotonous speed

A great day!
Rhythmical sound, she was swallowed up
By the underworld dwellers,
When she reached the catapulting apex
Again rose forth and dived deep

It stopped abruptly
And a clear, illuminating sky
With bright appearing and reappearing stars
In the now-time

"Turn back and go down
Until thy sunshine approaches to thee"
Monster-rail, bald and giant-handed being
Danced backwards, and vanished
It went high and whirled like 'Nza' bird
Dancing in living verse

28   It was torn like ashes of fire,
The justice was powerless to defend the inhabitant,
What are they to do?

He was chained to the bottom of sightless alley
The thorny path that demarcated the power of vision
A gloomy and shadowy aura
Was his companion

My clan, what antidote?
Where will I see to vacate?
Forward, the black power lives,
Backward, the misty watery presence stood
Like ashy goddess

The affair of his situation seemed
Like a tale from Ogbodiasa
And this was inevitable

He was on a mission of powerless fight;
The wave of rising vision striking

Forward and backward with force
When he returned the day was gone,

The night rendered impenetrable
What about my clan
My father's house gone?

A great tree trunk has fallen on its route,
The mud was scratched,
The lizards, with ants, working in the wood

If I go, please tell them that I was dead,
In the world of dream that seemed weird
They have done harm to me,
To go was impossible
To stay burnt to ashes

The riches of the fatherland,
Also vanishing?
If hell is what you want, what will it do?

Mutilate or chain me,
My people,
I am no longer alive,
What is life with inanimate body?

The blood of human turning to Ichor,
To rest was gone
And staying, endless
Oh, am I to see Segani again
And feel the cold embrace?

But each time,
Melting in thin air,
What is there to live here for?

When the light was gone
The playing moon no more
The crossbar was closed
And a stump was awaited,
But built, bit by bit,
To receive the fruit of survival .

www.ingramcontent.com/pod-product-compliance
Lightning Source LLC
Chambersburg PA
CBHW011957150426
43200CB00018B/2931